Super Crazy Fun

AF504542

BIG KID PHONICS

WARNING!

Lots of crazy words!

This textbook came about as the result of 20 years of trying to make kids enjoy learning English. It is designed around the use of the rhotic R and other characteristics of English pronunciation common in North America. We believe it can be used in other parts of the world as most phonics books can, and we are keen to hear feedback from anyone who tries this.

We want to make clear that the word "crazy" used in the title is in relation to any of the common definitions illustrated below, and does not refer in any way to the meaning "insane."

strange/illogical

wild

unexpected

fun

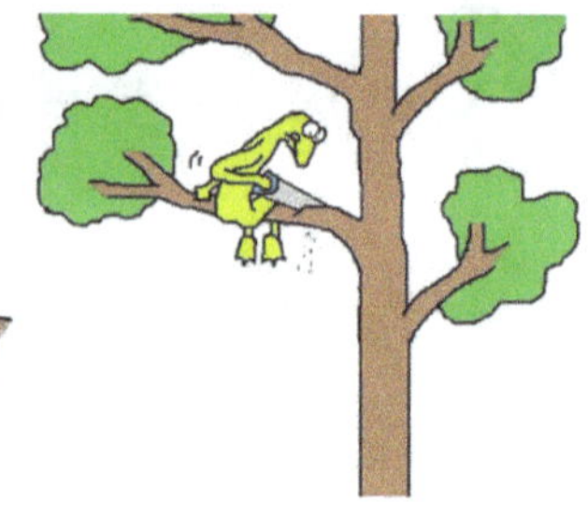

unwise

About the Authors:

Matthew Hitch has taught English in Korea for the better part of 20 years and holds a master's degree in applied linguistics. He clearly does not have a pig nose, and by most accounts is not at all malodorous. He also cuts a dashing figure according to his wife.

Sunok Moon prefers to go by the name Michelle, and is in fact quite scary as reported in the bio on the back of this book. She has a degree in English literature and has taught English in Korea for approximately 3 weeks longer than Matthew, who is writing this and finds it weird to refer to himself in the third person.

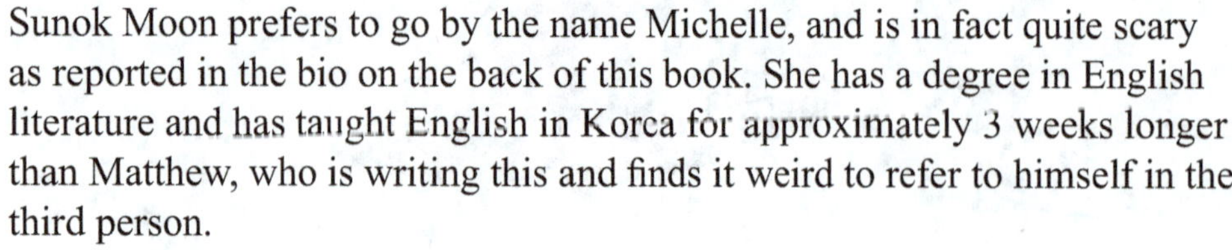

Contents

Welcome parents and teachers! ....page 2

Welcome students! ....page 4

The Alphabet ....page 6

Sounds ....page 10

Unit 1 A B C

alligator angry ant apple baby banana bird book candy car cat cup ....page 12

Unit 2 D E F

desk diamond dog door egg elbow elephant elf fish flower four frog.......................page 18

Unit 3 G H I

gold good gorilla grass happy hat hill house igloo ill in insect ....page 24

Unit 4 J K L

jail jam jet jump kangaroo key kick kite leg lemon lid lion ....page 30

Review ....page 36

More Sounds..page 40

Unit 5 M N O

milk monkey moon mouse nail nose nurse nut octopus old ostrich ox ....page 42

Unit 6 P Q R

pants peach poop potato queen question quick quiet radio red robot run ....page 48

Unit 7 S T U V

sad sit smell sun tear ten tiger time umbrella umpire under up van vest violin vomit ....page 54

Unit 8 W X Y Z

water wave window wish box fix fox six yawn yellow young yo yo zebra zero zipper zoo ....page 60

Review ....page 66

Test...page 72

Word List ....page 78

Our Sight Words & Flashcards ....page 82

Welcome parents and teachers!

Thank you for considering our book. Phonics books are notoriously boring, so this is the last bastion of publishing where even the tiniest bit of creativity can raise the bar (sorry phonics book publishers, but it's true). With that said, we humbly offer you our content. We have also intentionally challenged convention in a few ways. Much of what we have to say may be used or discarded though, and these books can be used just like any other mainstream phonics book. We hope you will choose to use whatever you please and dispose of the rest.

Please allow us to explain just where our method of teaching phonics may diverge from mainstream approaches, and please do forgive us for sharing information from what is undeniably the most mind-numbingly boring and seemingly useless field of study, linguistics. Most phonics books are not written by scholars in the field of linguistics. They are mostly written by early childhood educators, so perhaps that's the first divergence. We'll start with how we sound out consonants. In linguistic studies it is not uncommon for consonants to be distinguished by using a vowel (usually "ah") on both sides. This means a "V" sounds like "ahvah" and an "F" sounds like "ahfah" and so on. Most phonics books distinguish consonant sounds without such preceding vowel, but they do follow with a vowel in the form of the schwa. This is fine for most consonants, but the ones that are able to be maintained until breath is exhausted can be confusing with a schwa where they end a word. It's mostly ESL students who feel this confusion, but we think it doesn't hurt to teach those consonants without a schwa to native speakers as well, so where "V" sounds like "və" in most phonics books, in our book it is presented as "vvvvvvv" with no schwa. We apply this to all long consonant sounds in our audio files (L,M,N&R are also presented as long with a tiny schwa sound at the end though). If you have read this far, we take our hats off to you. Most would be fast asleep by now.

The next divergence is our use of Magic E. We chose Magic E for the fun potential. The Split Digraphs just can't seem to hold a crowd. Magic E is no longer used in most educational settings for many reasons, but mostly because as a rule it cannot be defined clearly. We do mention that split digraphs are better though, mainly to extend an olive branch to all the teachers we hope will buy our books.

And the final divergence we would like to mention is our choice of words. Our choice of words may seem a bit odd at times throughout the books, but we chose them for their potential for keeping kids engaged over their usefulness. We approach a phonics book as a tool to teach about sounds much more than vocabulary. Poop, vomit, spit, fart, snot, and burp are the most popular with our students. We tried to find a spot for booger, but alas...

Our word choice is also strange in that it includes words that have the long E vowel when teaching split digraphs. Most phonics books glance over the long E vowel. The argument we have heard for this is that it is difficult for the younger students, but we suspect that it's avoided more because it's difficult for authors to find suitable words. We decided to give it a try, and our experience is that the long E words we chose are not that difficult for our students to grasp. Given that English is their second language, we believe native English speaking kids will cope with them just fine. Also you may notice our sight words are not all actually sight words - oops! Anyway, we hope you enjoy our silly books.

Welcome students!

Hello. I am a gorilla. Together we are going to
make a lot of very silly faces and sounds!

Hello. I am an elephant. I am a
little wide. Some letters are also
a little wide. You will see me
around them!

Hello. I am a lizard. I am a little thin. Some letters are also a little thin. You will see me around them!

Hello. I am a mole. I like to dig! Some letters also like to dig. You will see me around them!

Hello. I am a pig. I don't care about letters. I just hang around.

I am a fly. I am smelly. You will see me around smelly stuff.

Let's get started...

The Alphabet

A B C D E

F G H I J

K L M N O

P Q R S T

U V W X Y

Z z z z z z z

Tracks 1-9

Sing along:

A B C D E F G~
H I J K L M N ~
O P Q..

Track 7

No, no!   It has to rhyme!

A B C D E F G ~
H I J K L-M-N-O-P ~
Q R S T U V ~
W X Y & Z

The Alphabet

The Written Alphabet

Writing has rules. If we don't follow them we might seem a bit silly! But then again, it's okay to be a bit silly sometimes, isn't it?

We should write all letters on the line, but small g, j, p, q, and y go under the line a little, like a mole digging a hole!

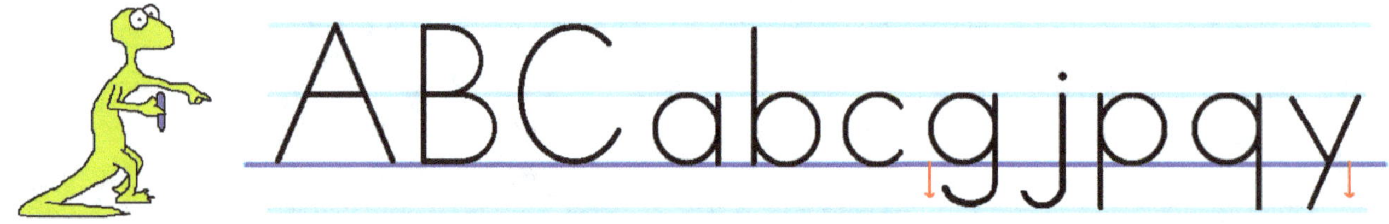

Vertical lines go down, and horizontal lines go left to right! All circles are are counter-clockwise, except circles connected to the righthand side of a line. Dots and crossing lines are last!

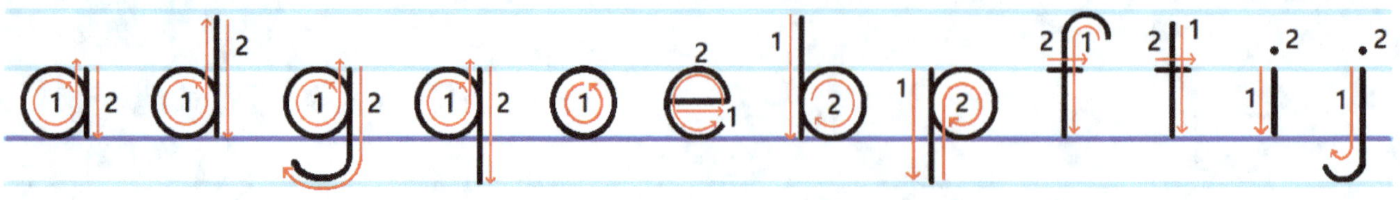

The Alphabet

The typed Alphabet

Typed letters can be a bit confusing. Sometimes there are extra curls or lines missing. We think these four are the most important ones for you to know:

a = a

g = g

I = l

t = t

Your Writing

We don't like to tell people how to write, but we want the best for you, so we show you these writing rules. You can use them if you wish.
Your style can be however you like:

My name is David

My name is David

Sounds

Vowels

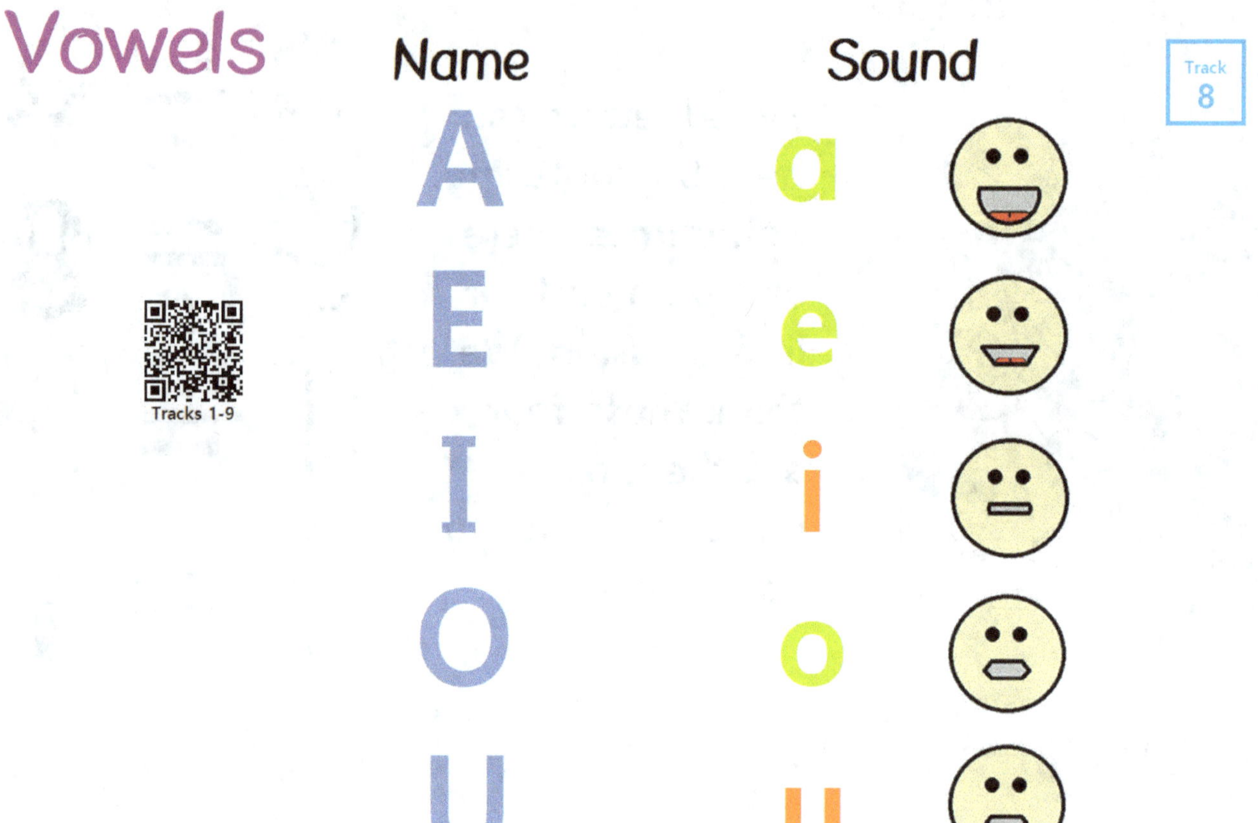

The name is long. The sound is short. i and u are VERY short.

Long and short sounds

Some letters can make a long sound, and some letters definitely can't! It's mportant to know which ones can make a long sound. We'll be learning that.

Sounds

"Sometimes Sounds"

Many letters have a "sometimes sound."
Sometimes the letter A makes the same
sound as the letter U!
You can hear it in the word "banana."
We use that sometimes sound for the word "a."

And sometimes U and O
make the same sound!

It's very strange, isn't it?

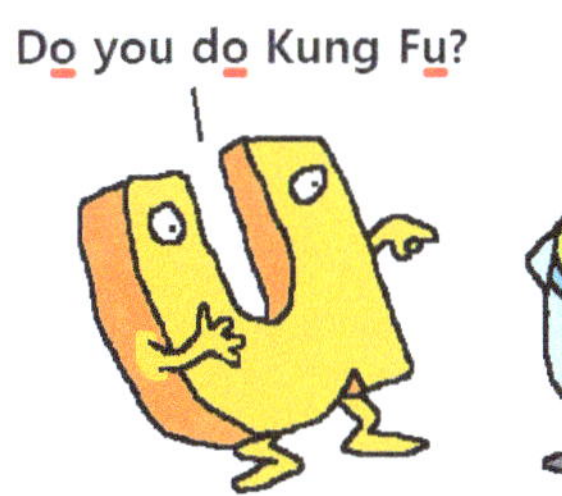

Practice with your teacher:

1. 

A banana

2. 

A cobra

3. 

A panda

4. 

A puma

Listen, point, and make the sound

A a   B b   C c

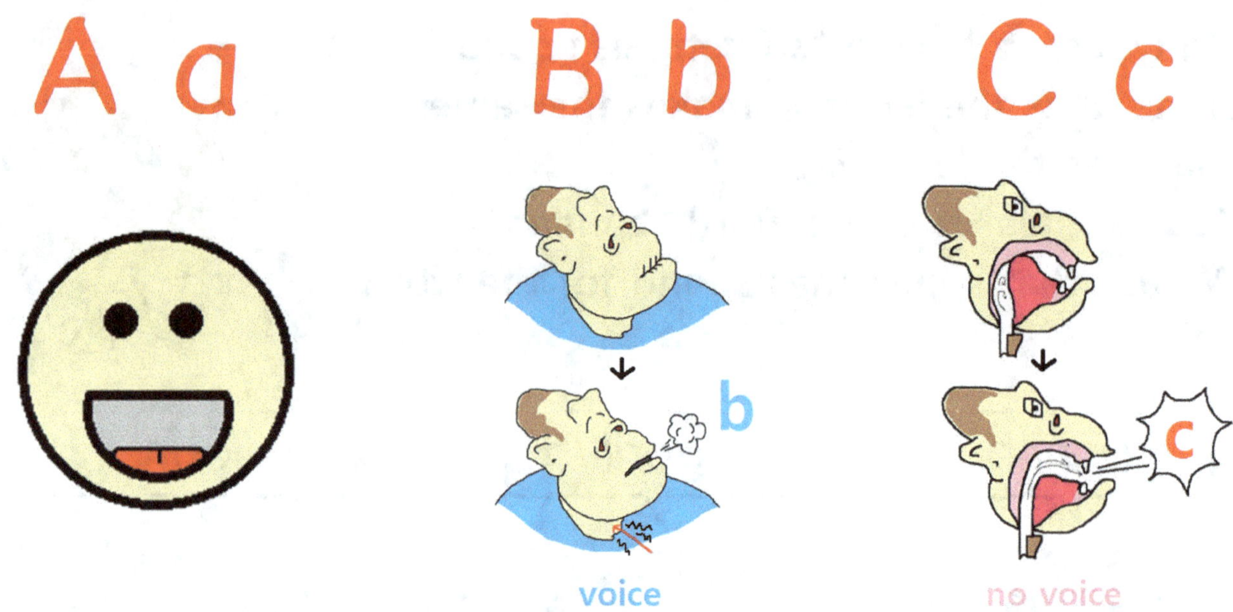

Listen and draw a line from the sound to the matching picture

a   b   c

Follow the rules

A  a

B b

C c

New Words

Tracks 10-19

Listen, point and repeat the new words 

Track 13

Aa

Bb

Cc

Do it again..and again.. and again!

Exercises

Writing practice

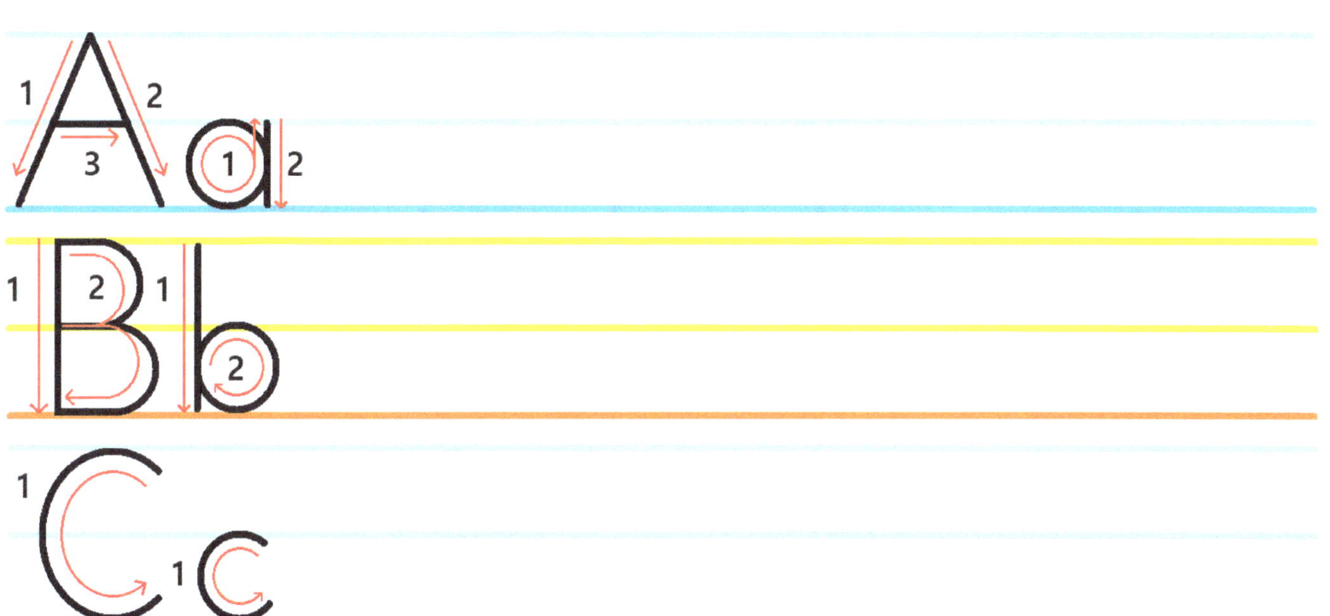

Word search   *Listen and circle the word you hear*

Track 14

Tracks 10-19

Exercises

Circle the word you hear

Track 15

Tracks 10-19

Write the matching letter

Chant

Track 16

Sight words: a / an   and

An apple and a banana,
An apple and a banana,
An apple and a banana,
And an angry cat.

A cup and candy,
A cup and candy,
A cup and candy,
And an angry bird.

Story

Circle the sound you hear

1 a   b   c   2 a   b   c

3 a   b   c   4 a   b   c

5 a   b   c   6 a   b   c

Listen and read along

UNIT 2   Single-Letter Sounds

Listen, point, and make the sound  

D d   E e   F f

Listen and draw a line from the sound to the matching picture

d   e   f

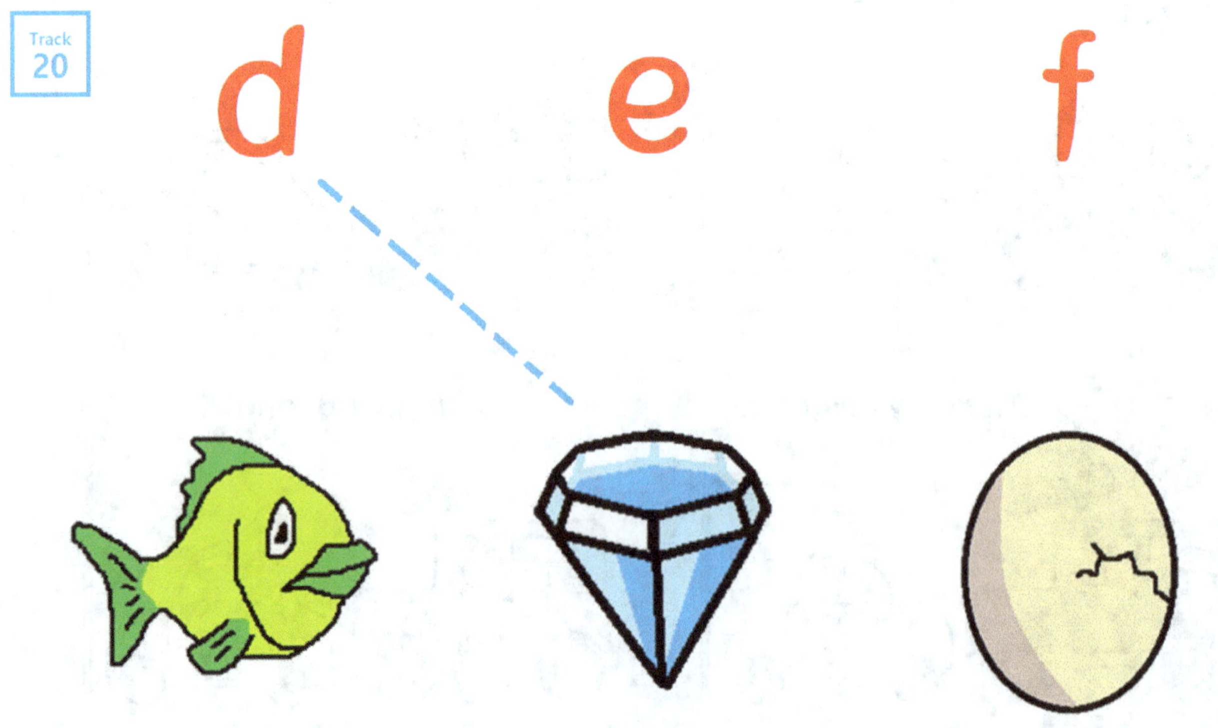

Follow the rules

D  d

E e

F f

New Words

Listen, point and repeat the new words 
Track 21

Dd

desk   diamond   dog   door

Ee

egg   elbow   elephant   elf

Ff

fish   flower   four   frog

Do it again..and again.. and again!

Exercises

Writing practice

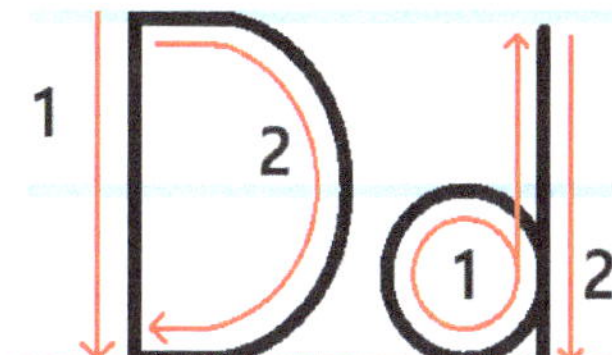

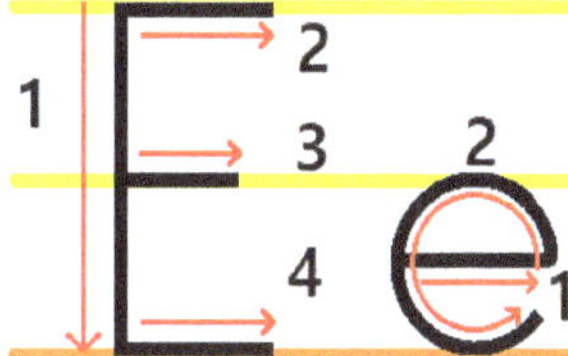

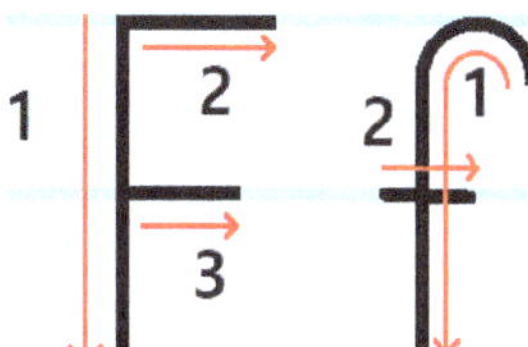

Word search *Listen and circle the word you hear*

Tracks 20-29

desk   diamond   four   fish   flower   elephant

elbow   elf   dog   frog   door   egg

Exercises

Circle the word you hear

Track 23

Tracks 20-29

1

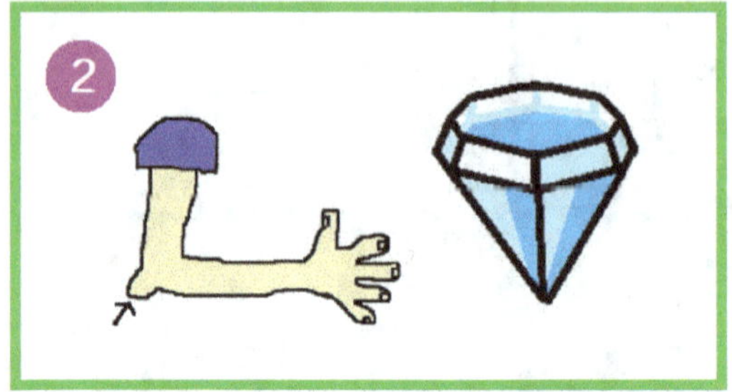

2

3

4

Write the matching letter

Chant

Track 24

New sight words: all   on

A fish and a frog,
And an elephant elbow,
All on a diamond desk.

A book and a cup,
And an angry ant,
All on a diamond desk.

22   Unit 2

Story

Circle the sound you hear

Track 25

Tracks 20-29

1. d e f 　 2. d e f

3. d e f 　 4. d e f

5. d e f 　 6. d e f

Listen and read along

Track 26

New sight words:　in　the

An elf in the flowers.

A dog in the flowers.

A dog-egg in the flowers.

An elf in the dog-egg!

Listen, point, and make the sound  

G g   H h   I i

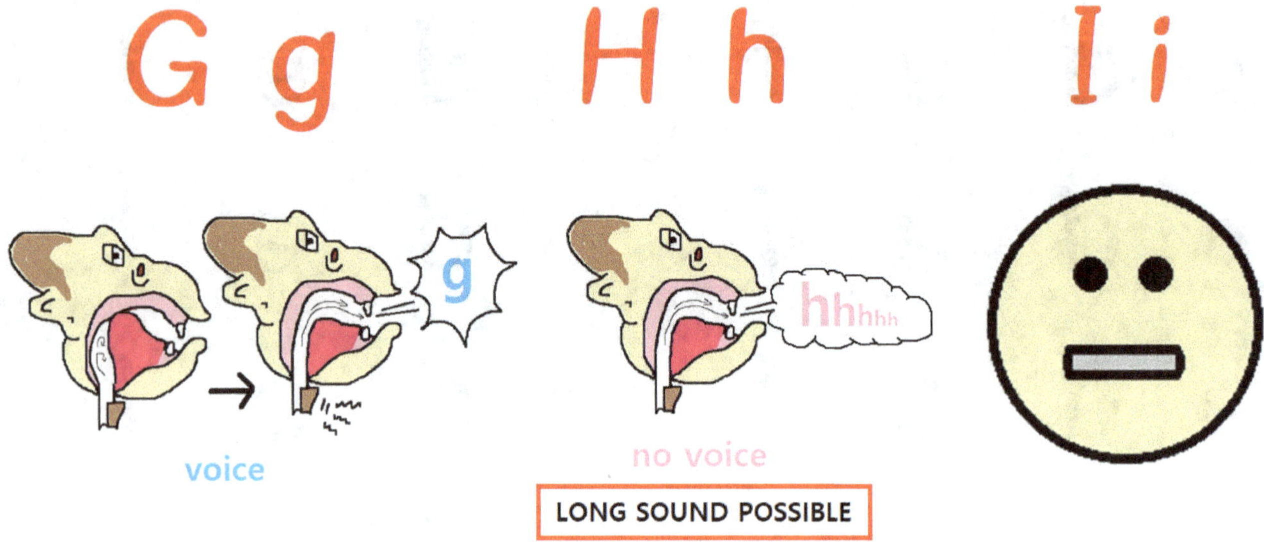

Listen and draw a line from the sound to the matching picture

g   h   i

Follow the rules

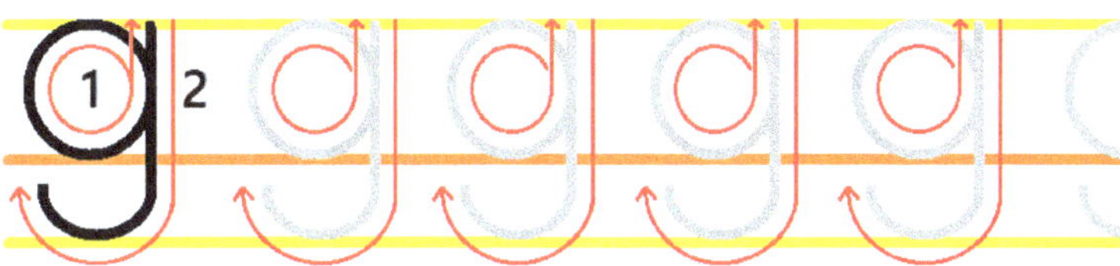

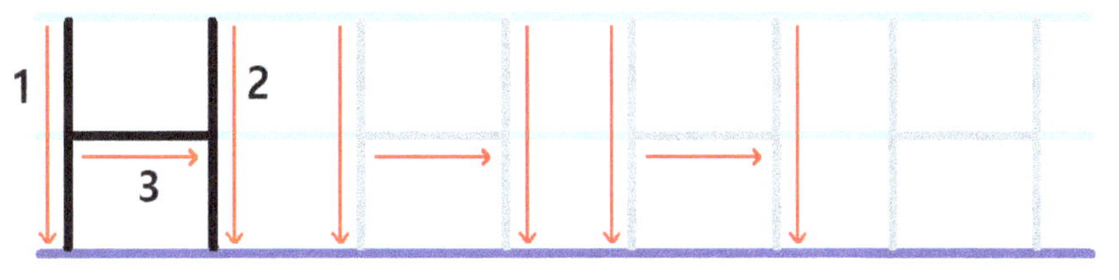

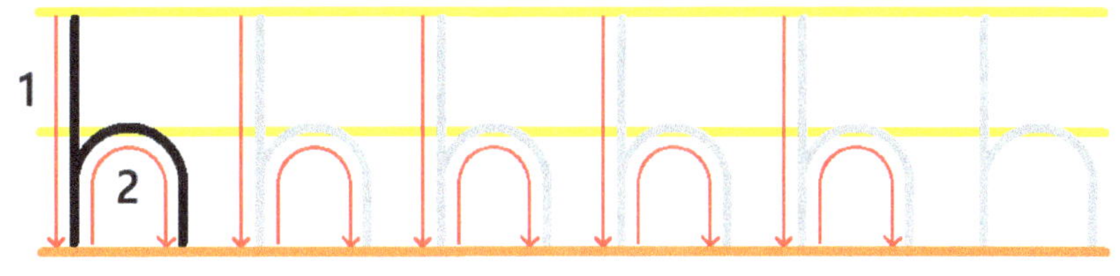

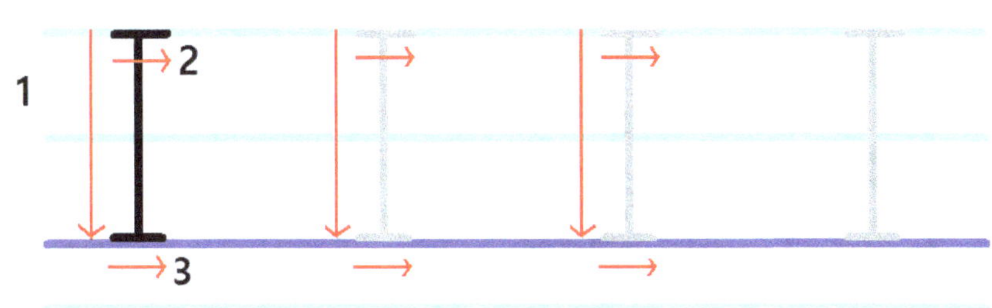

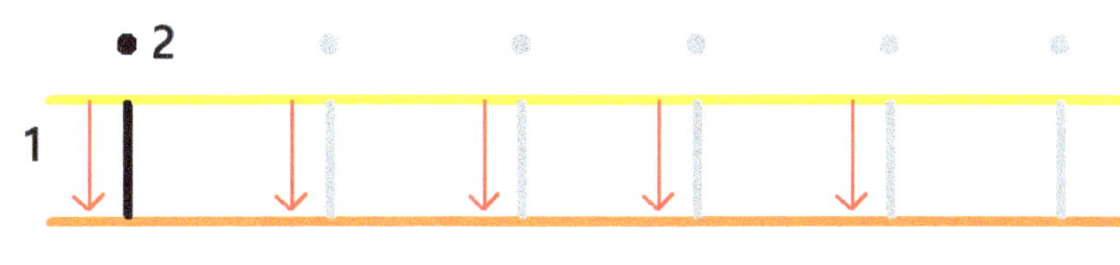

Listen, point and repeat the new words

Gg

| gold | good | gorilla | grass |

Hh

| happy | hat | hill | house |

Ii

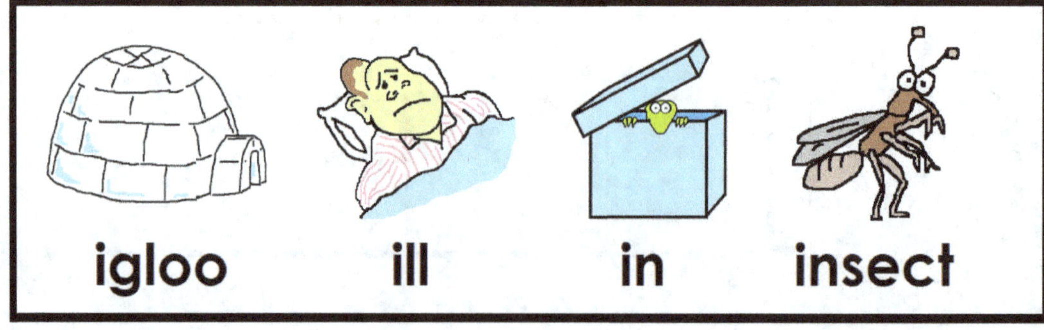

| igloo | ill | in | insect |

Do it again..and again.. and again!

Exercises

Writing practice

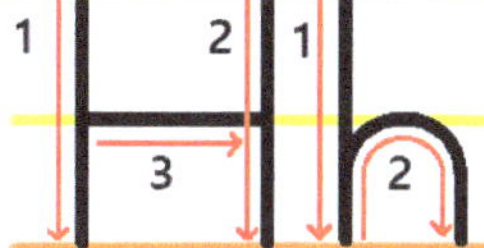

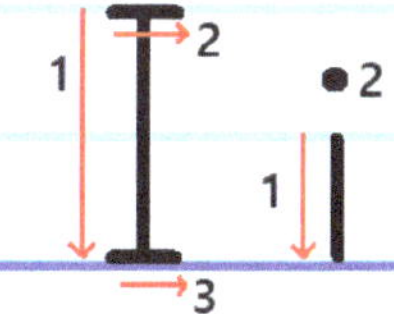

Word search   Listen and circle the word you hear

Tracks 30-39

in   **good**   **happy**   **grass**   **ill**   **house**

gorilla   **hat**   **igloo**   **hill**   **gold**   **insect**

Exercises

Circle the word you hear

Tracks 30-39

Write the matching letter

Chant

Ill in a hat,
Ill in a good hat,
Ill in a good gold hat.

Ill in a house,
Ill in a good house,
Ill in a good gold house.

Circle the sound you hear

Track 33

Tracks 30-39

1. g h i
2. g h i
3. g h i
4. g h i
5. g h i
6. g h i

Listen and read along

Track 34

New sight words: no

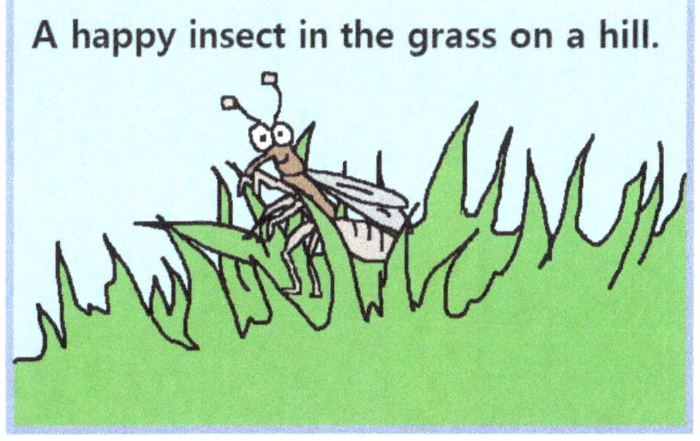

Listen, point, and make the sound

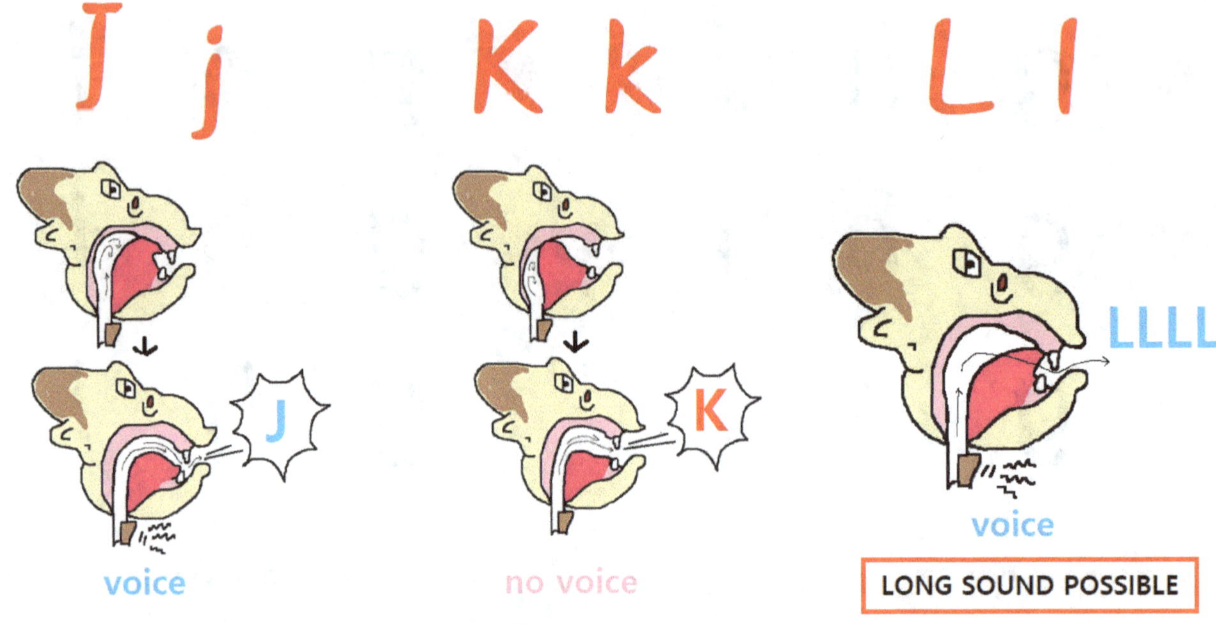

Listen and draw a line from the sound to the matching picture

Follow the rules

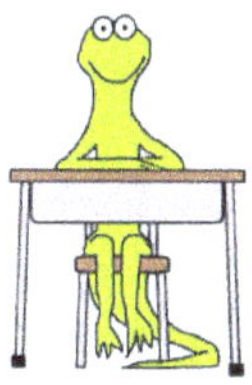

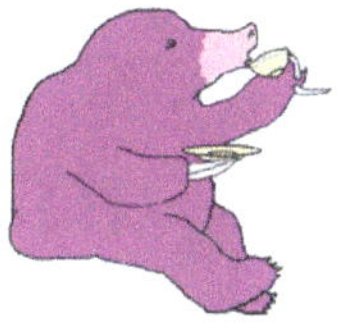

J

j

K

k

L

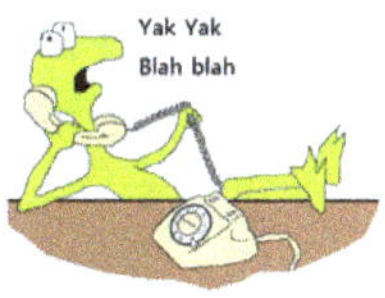

l

New Words

Tracks 30-39

Track 37

J j

jail   jam   jet   jump

K k

kangaroo   key   kick   kite

L l

leg   lemon   lid   lion

Writing practice

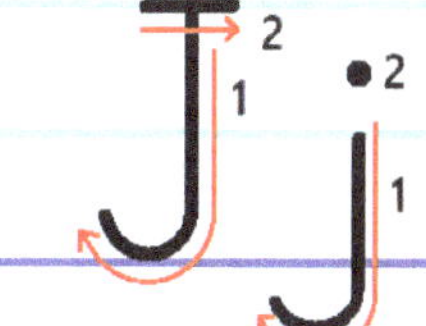

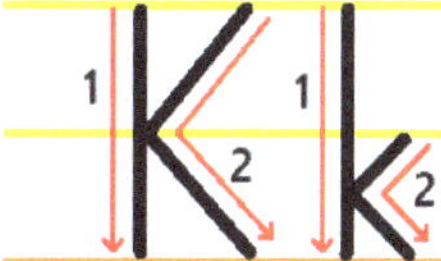

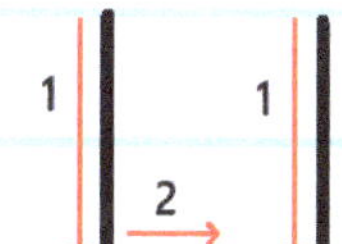

Word search Listen and circle the word you hear

Track 38

Tracks 30-39

Exercises

Circle the word you hear

Tracks 30-39

Write the matching letter

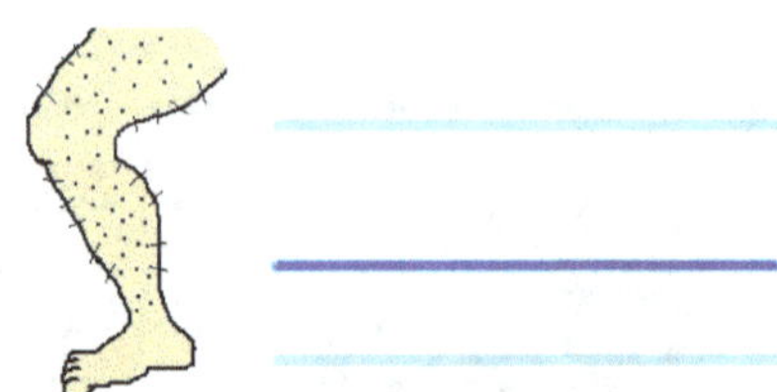

Chant

New sight words: lift   like

Lemon jam,
Lemon jam,
Lift the lid,
Kangaroos like lemon jam.

Kangaroo jam,
Kangaroo jam,
Lift the lid,
Lions like kangaroo jam.

34   Unit 4

Story

Circle the sound you hear

Tracks 40-49

1 j k l   **2** j k l

3 j k l   **4** j k l

5 j k l   **6** j k l

Listen and read along

New sight words: get

Lion and kangaroo in jail.

Kick the leg! Get the key!

Jump in the jet!

Lion in jail.

Review

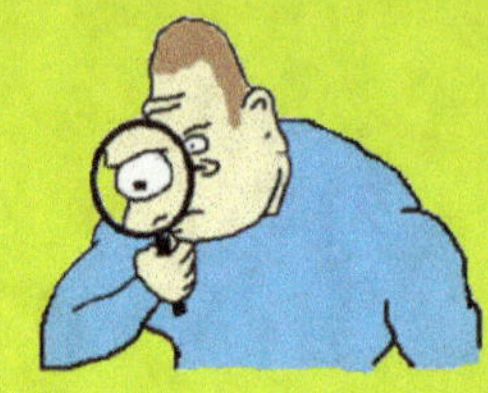

Tracks 40-49

Track 43

Listen, point, and say

A a 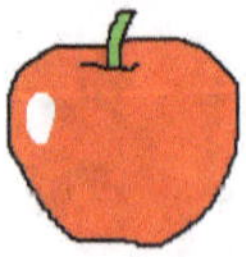

B b 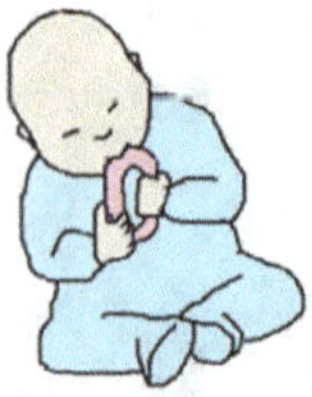

C c 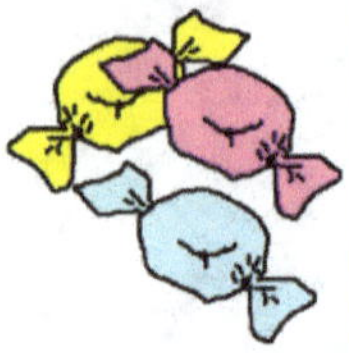

D d 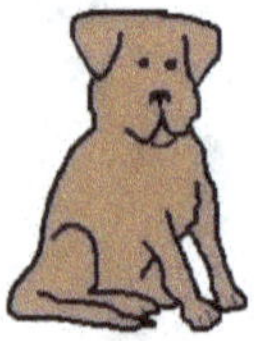

E e 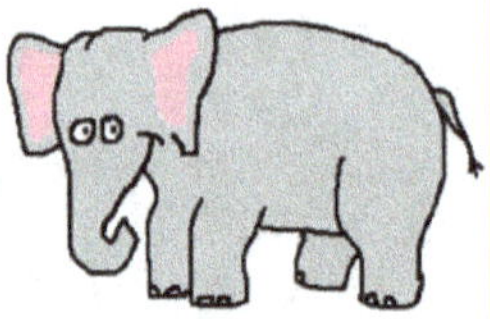

F f 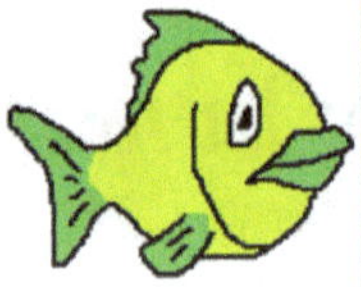

G g 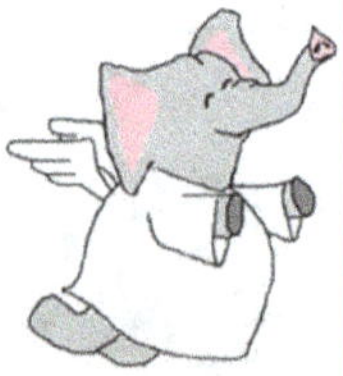

H h 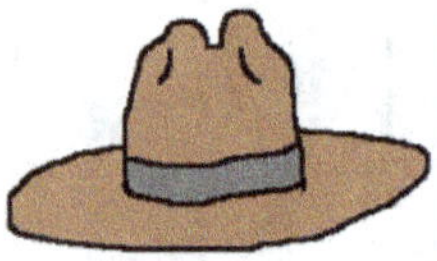

I i 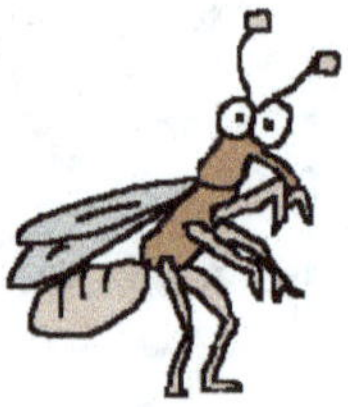

J j 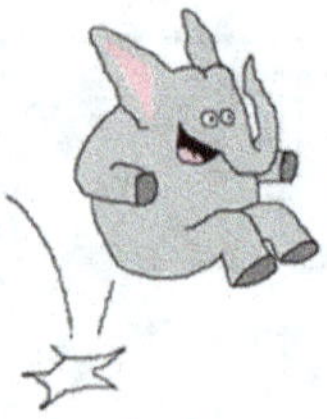

K k 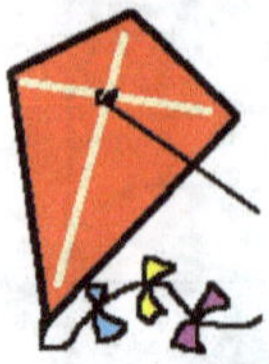

L l 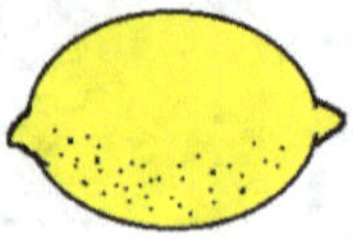

Review

Say all the words and write the letters

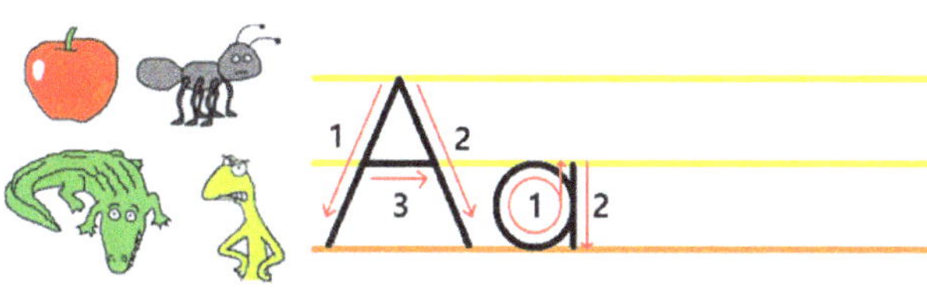 Aa 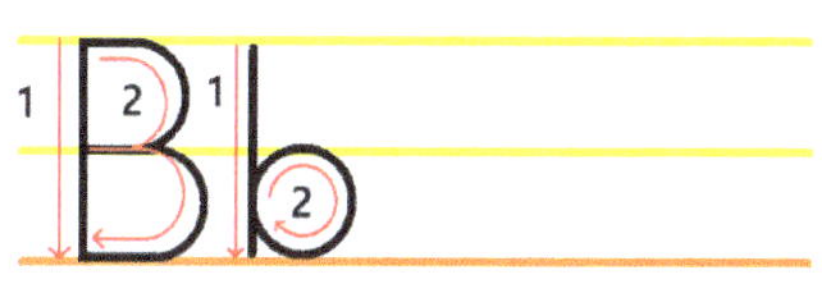 Bb

 Cc 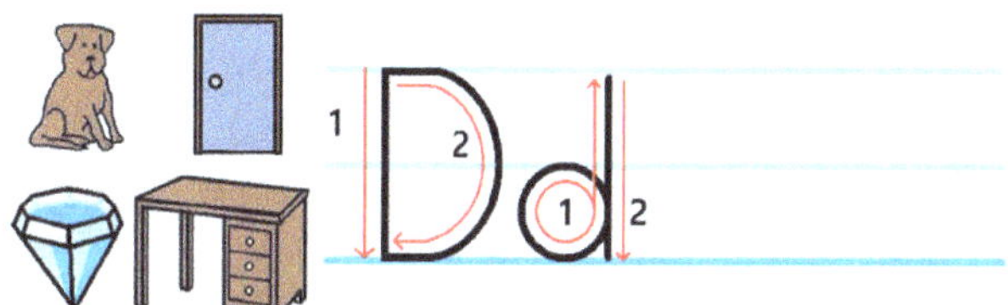 Dd

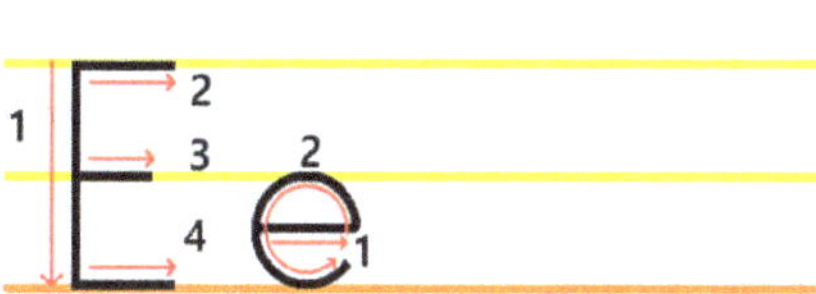 Ee 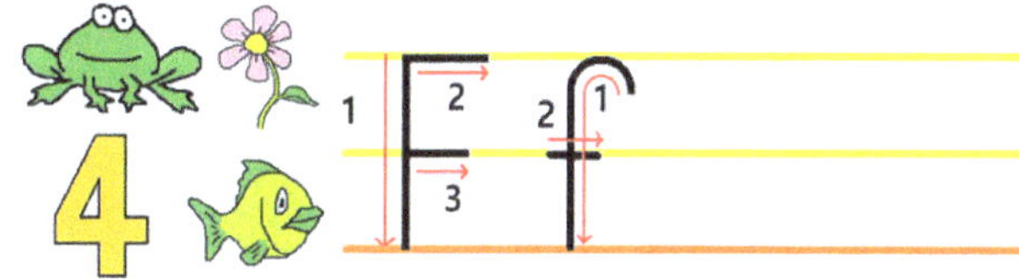 Ff

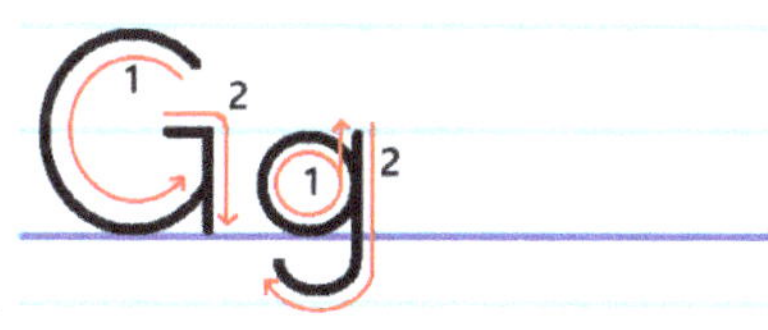 Gg 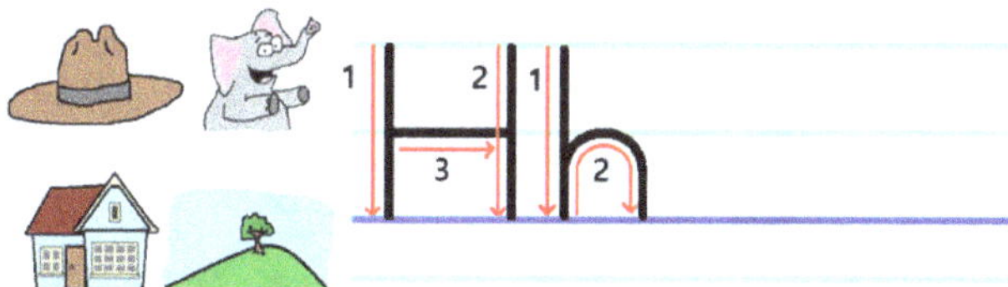 Hh

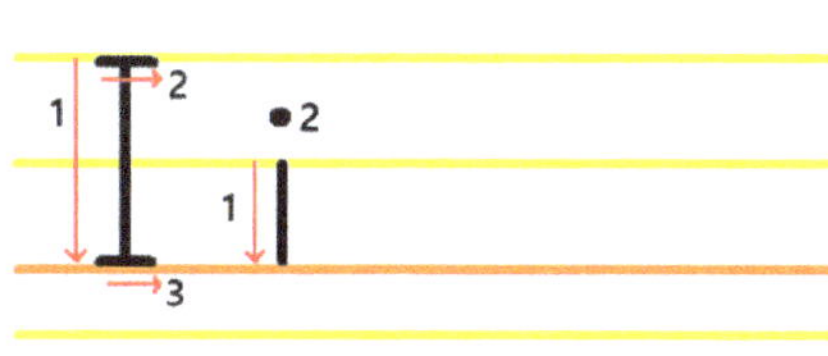 Ii 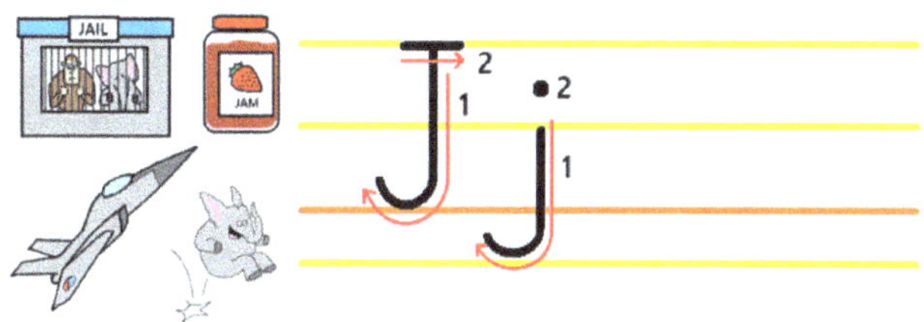 Jj

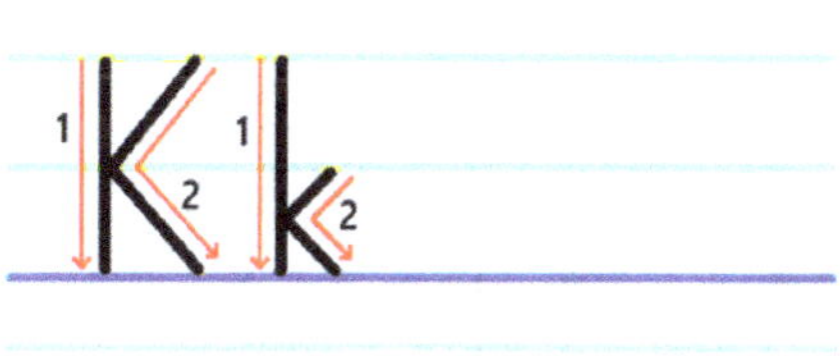 Kk 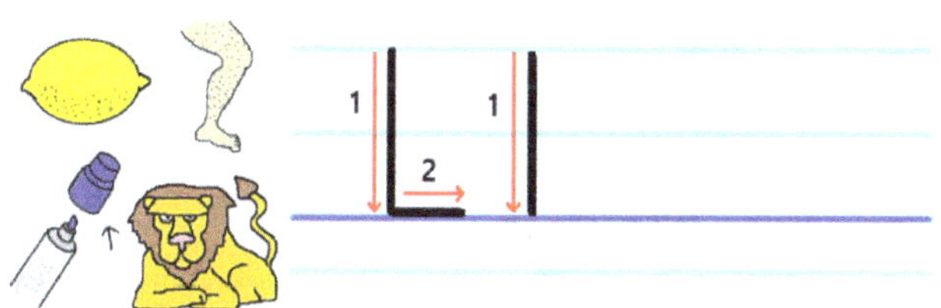 Ll

Review

Find the path

1 H   a

2 A   h

3 G   d

4 D   g

Listen and circle the matching letter

1  d e f	2  i h j
3  i g k	4  j k l
5 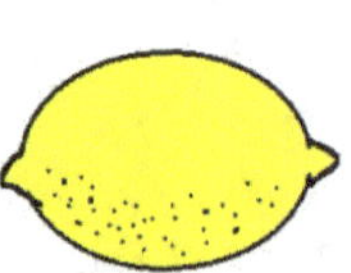 a c f	6  d h b
7  g b a	8  e l c

Review

Listen and circle. Then write the word

Tracks 40-49

1      

2      

3      

4      

5      

"Sometimes Sounds"

Track 46

Tracks 40-49

Sometimes when a vowel begins a word, we use its name, not its sound.

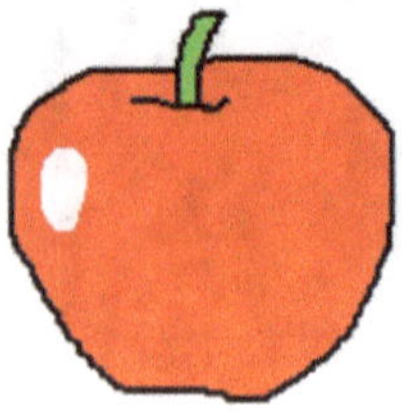

apple   acorn

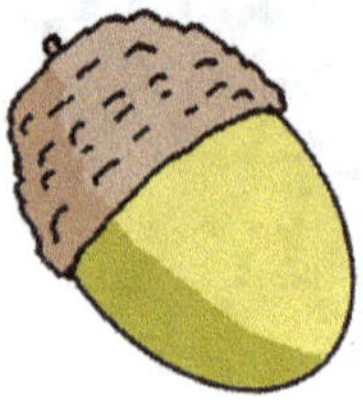

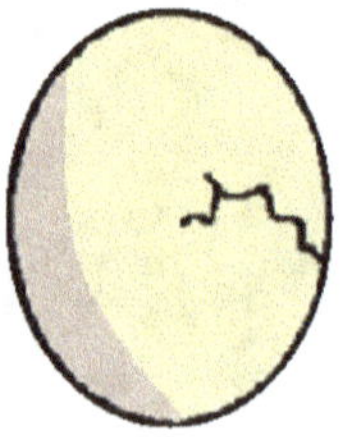

egg   eagle

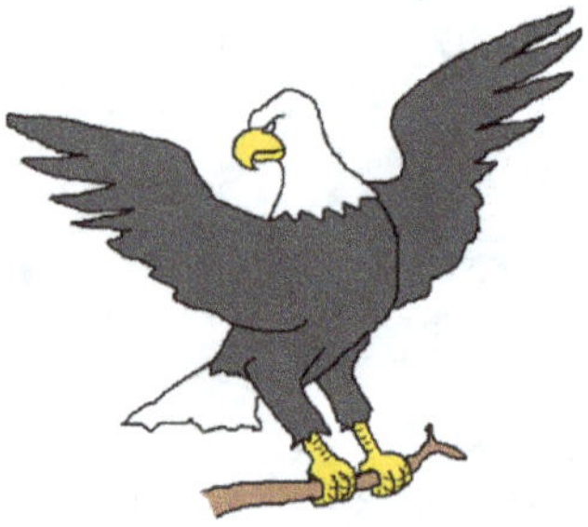

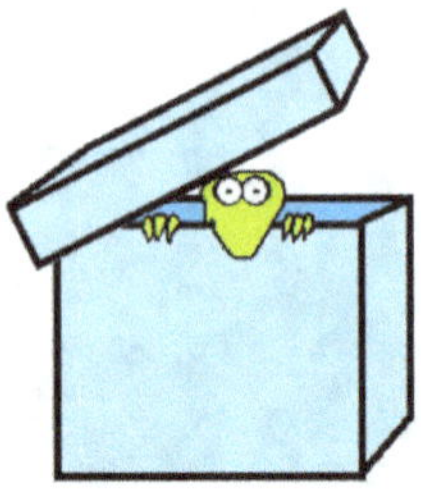

in   ice-cream

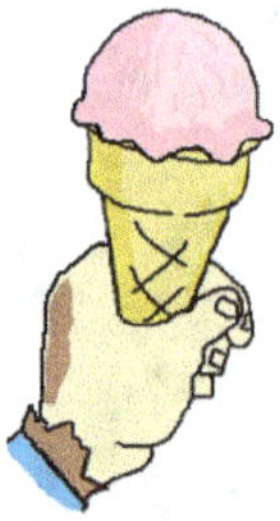

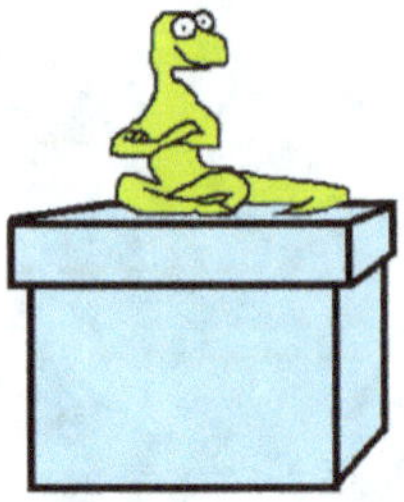

on   old

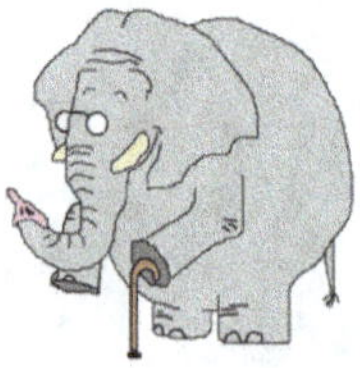

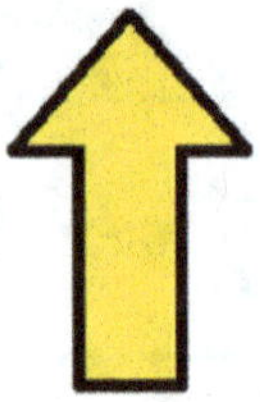

up   unicorn

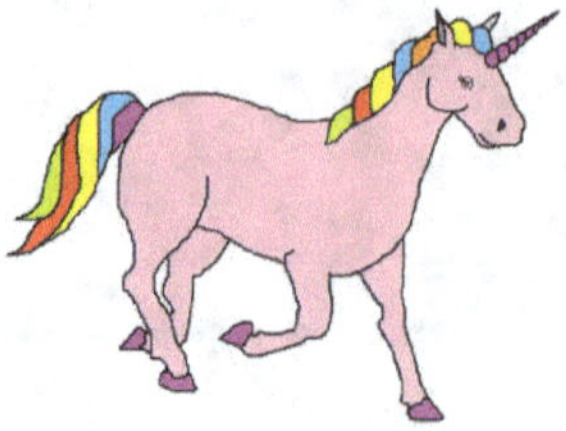

More Sounds

Syllables

Have you noticed that words have a rythm?

"Banana" has 3 beats, but we don't say "beats" for words. We say "syllables."

(Not silly bulls)

Not everyone uses the same syllables...or even SPELLING!

cam/er/a

camera

aer/o/plane

air/plane

di/a/mond

diamond

Listen, point, and make the sound

M m   N n   O o

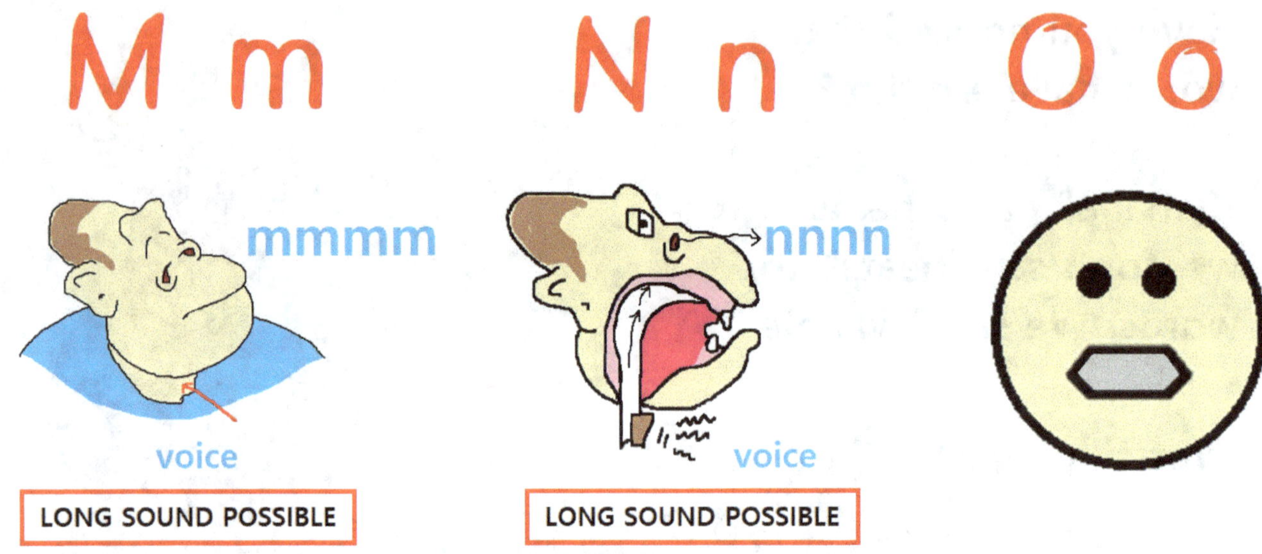

Listen and draw a line from the sound to the matching picture

m   n   o

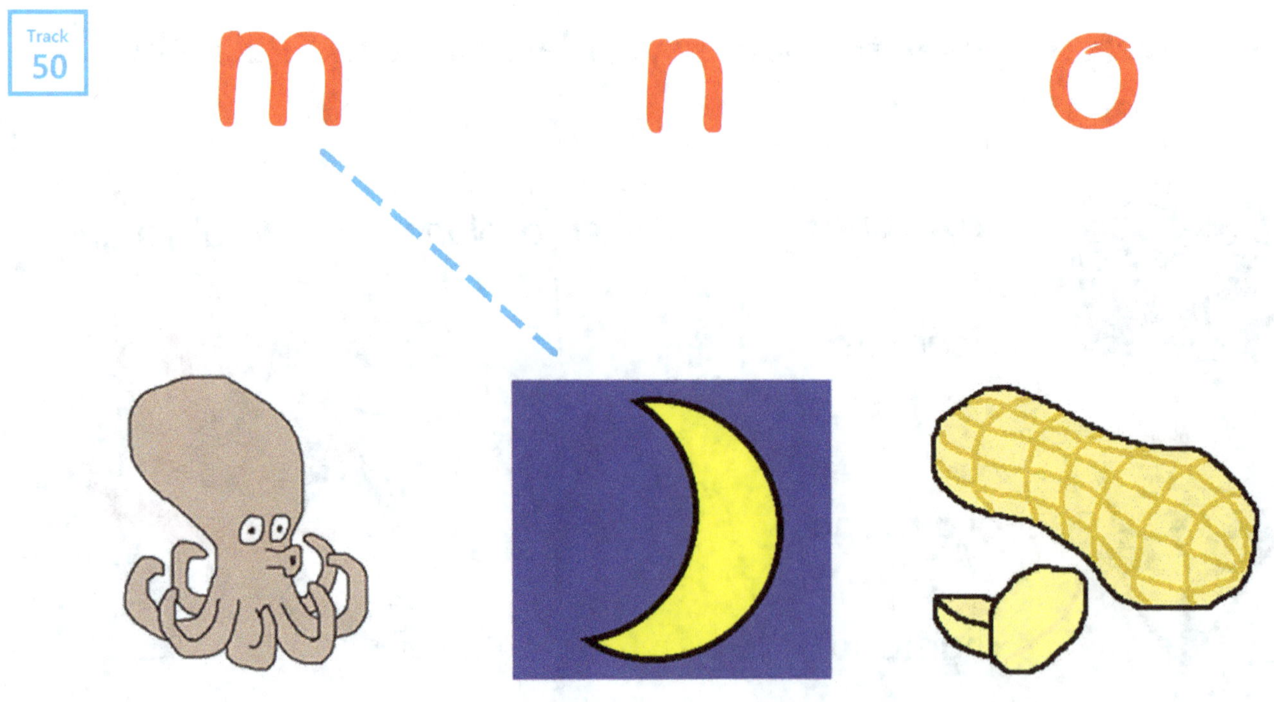

Follow the rules

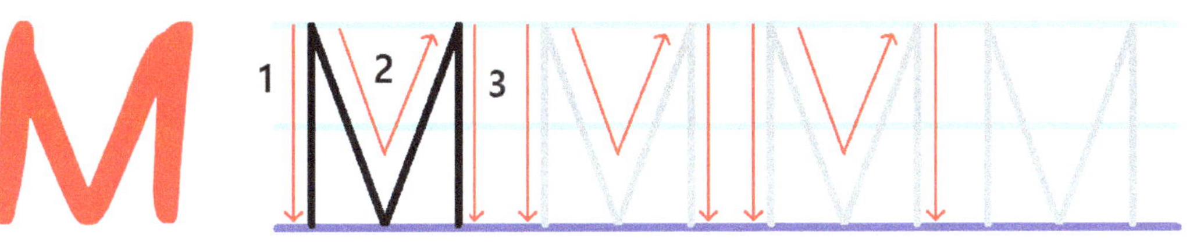

M

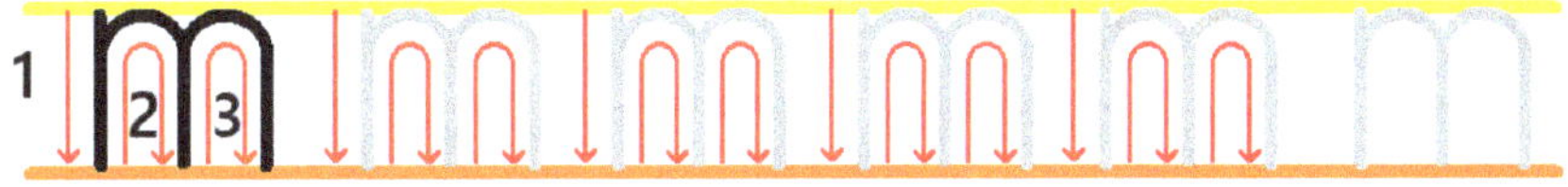

m

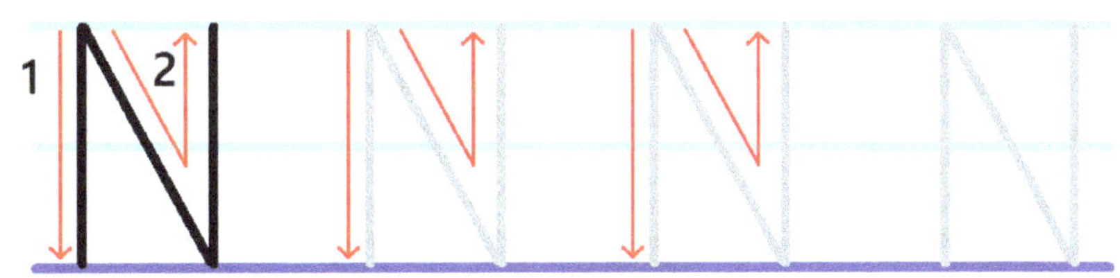

N

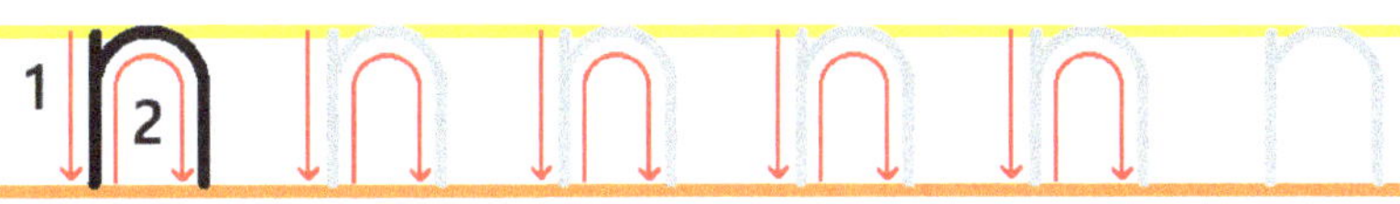

n

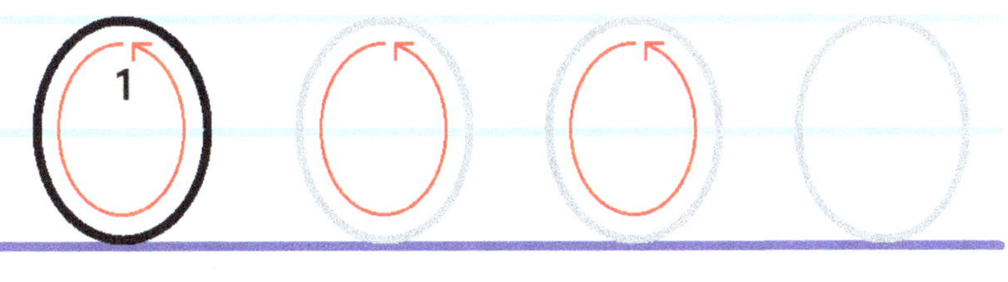

O

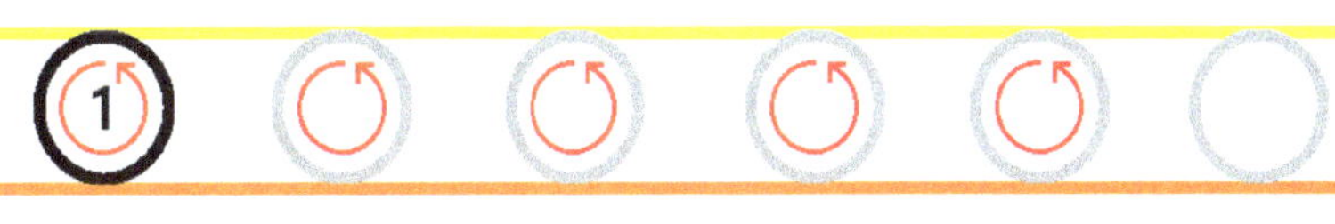

o

New Words

Tracks 50-59

Listen, point and repeat the new words 
Track 51

Mm

milk   **monkey**   **moon**   **mouse**

Nn

 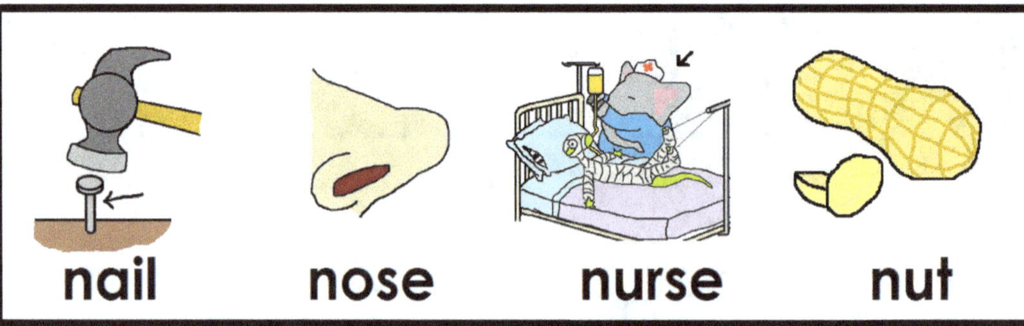

nail   **nose**   **nurse**   **nut**

Oo

 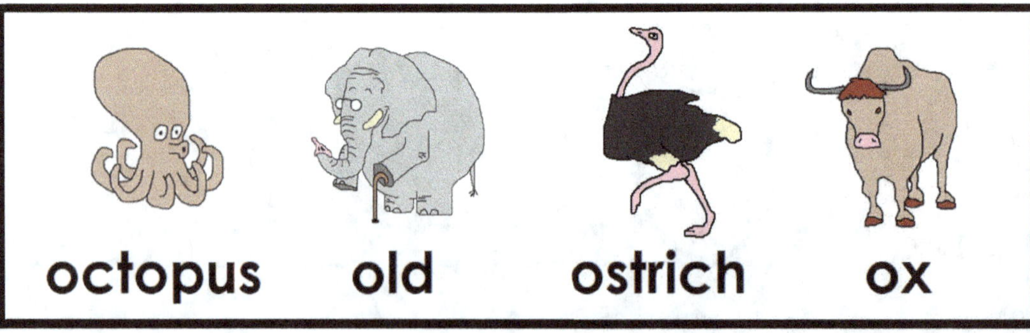

octopus   **old**   **ostrich**   **ox**

Do it again..and again.. and again!

Exercises

Writing practice

Word search *Listen and circle the word you hear*

octopus   milk   ox   ostrich   nut   monkey

nail   old   nurse   moon   nose   mouse

Exercises

Circle the word you hear

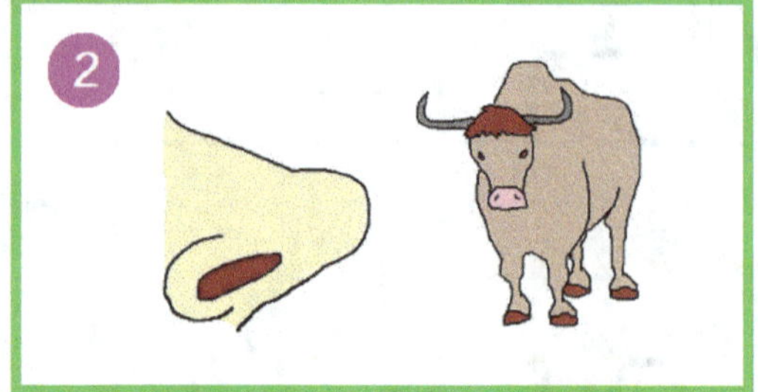

Write the matching letter

 ____________

 ____________

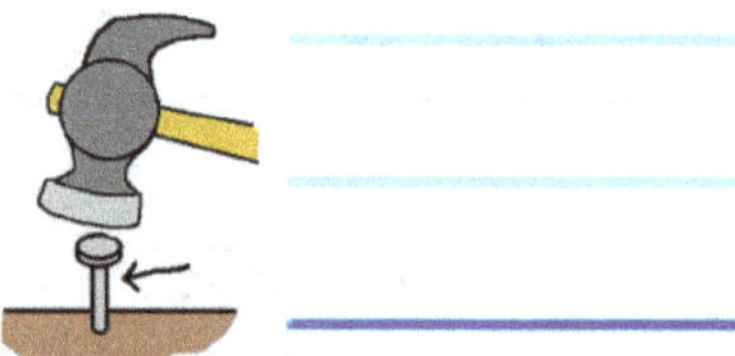 ____________

Chant

New sight words: oh   not

Old monkey milk,
And an octopus nose.

Old monkey milk,
And an octopus nose.

Oh no! Oh no!
Not old monkey milk!!

Story

Circle the sound you hear

1. m n o   2. m n o

3. m n o   4. m n o

5. m n o   6. m n o

Listen and read along

Ox and mouse and ostrich on the moon.

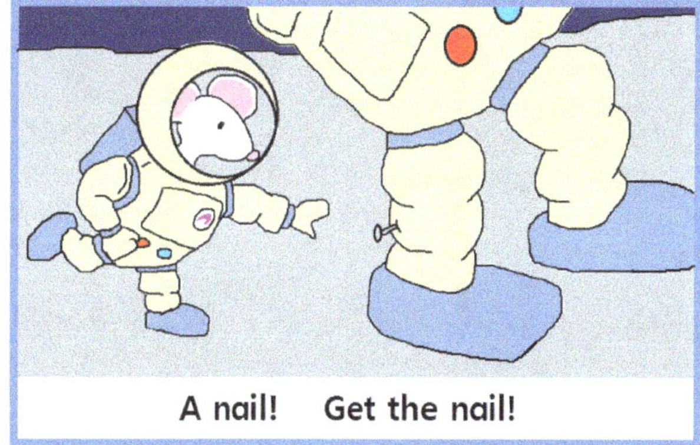

A nail!   Get the nail!

Oh no. Not good.

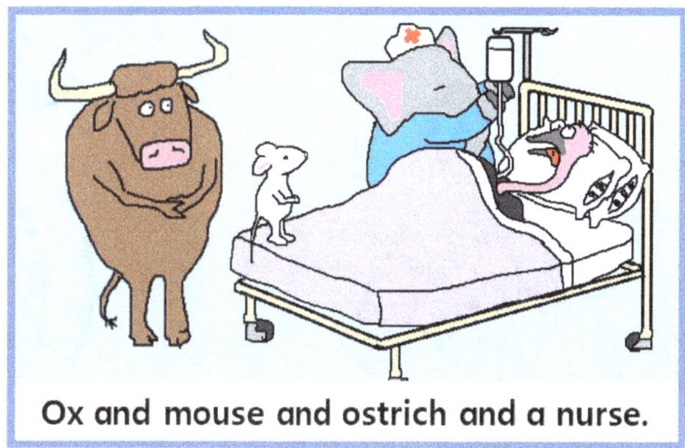

Ox and mouse and ostrich and a nurse.

UNIT 6　Single-Letter Sounds

Listen, point, and make the sound  

Track 57

Tracks 50-59

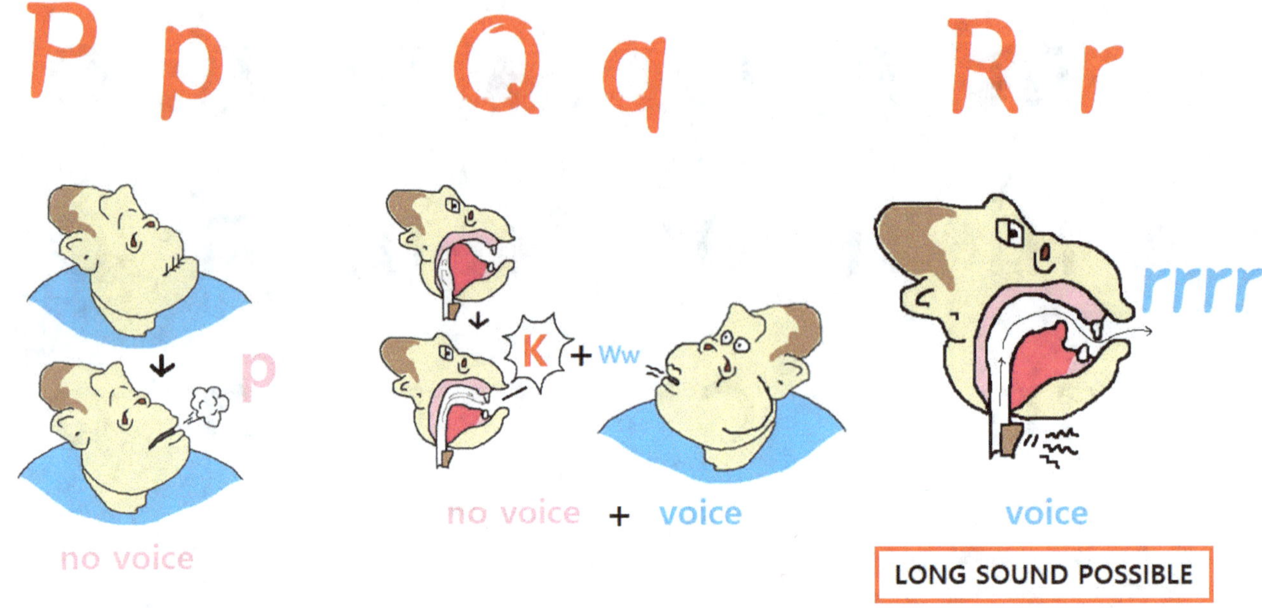

Listen and draw a line from the sound to the matching picture

Track 58

p　　q　　r

Follow the rules

P

p

Q

q

R

r

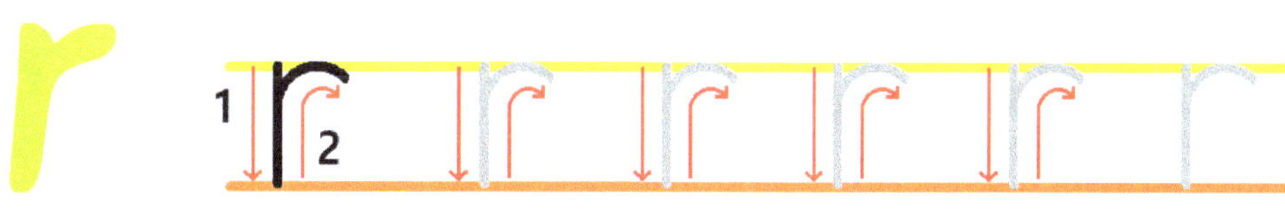

Listen, point and repeat the new words

Tracks 50-59

Pp

pants   peach   poop   potato

Qq

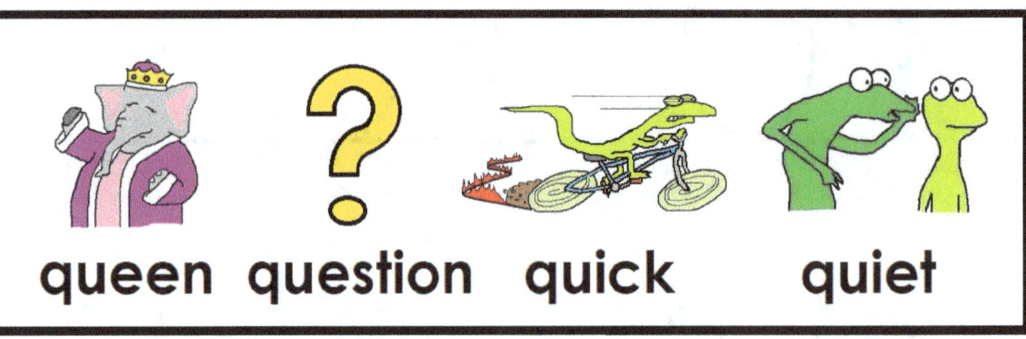

queen   question   quick   quiet

Rr

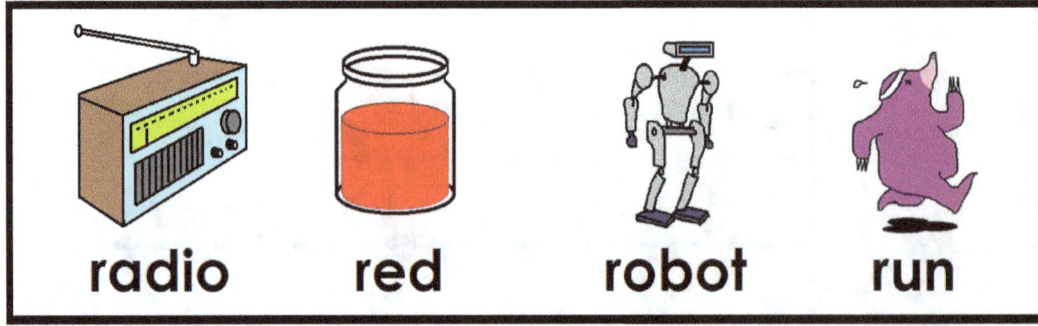

radio   red   robot   run

Do it again.. and again.. and again!

Writing practice

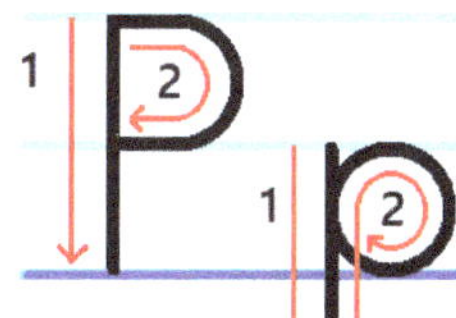

Word search *Listen and circle the word you hear*

Track 60

Tracks 60-69

Exercises

Circle the word you hear

Tracks 60-69

Track 61

1

2

3

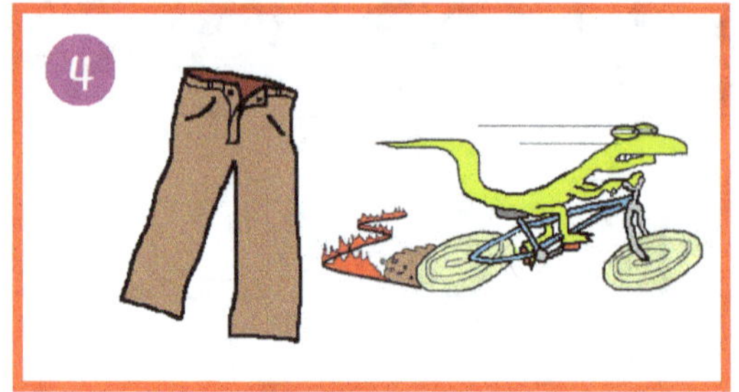

4

Write the matching letter

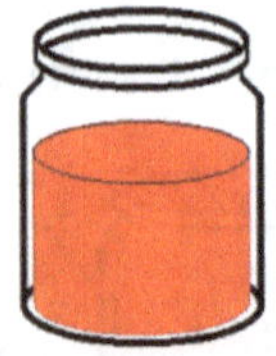

?

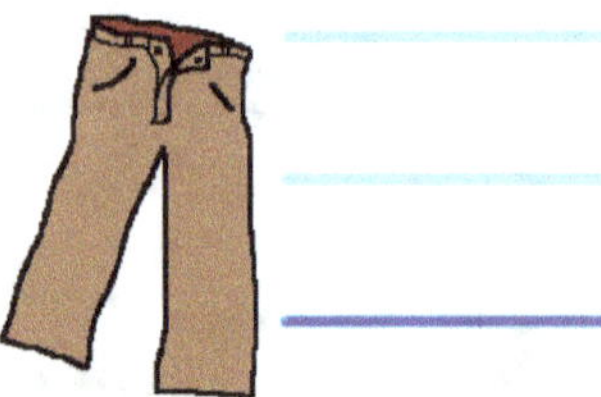

Chant

Track 62

New sight words: did   you   your   yes   my

A quick quiet question:
Did you poop your pants?

A quick quiet question:
Did you poop your pants?

Yes, I did. Yes I did.
I did poop my pants.

Story

Circle the sound you hear

Tracks 60-69

1. p   q   r
2. p   q   r
3. p   q   r
4. p   q   r
5. p   q   r
6. p   q   r

Listen and read along

New sight words: has   put

UNIT 7   Single-Letter Sounds

Listen, point, and make the sound

Tracks 60-69

Track 65

S s   T t   U u   V v

Listen and draw a line from the sound to the matching picture

s   t   u   v

Track 66

New Words

Tracks 60-69

Track 67

Ss

| sad | sit | smell | sun |

Tt

| tear | ten | tiger | time |

Uu

| umbrella | umpire | under | up |

Vv

| van | vest | violin | vomit |

Do it again..and again.. and again!

Exercises

Writing practice

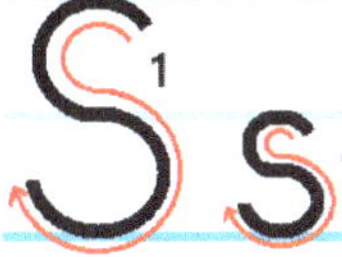 S s

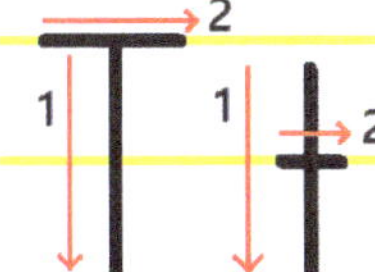 T t

 U u

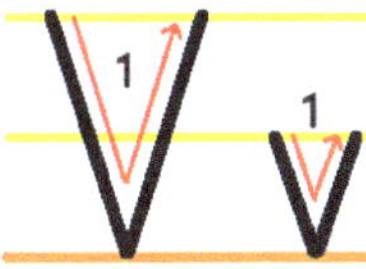 V v

Word search *Listen and circle the word you hear*

Tracks 60-69

     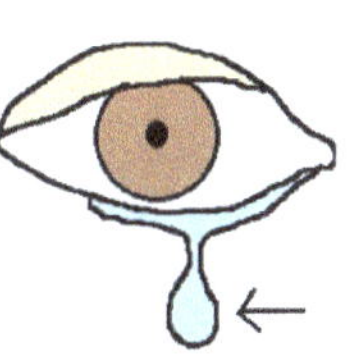

sad	under	up	ten	vest	van	smell	tear

sit	time	sun	umbrella	tiger	vomit	violin	umpire

Exercises

Circle the word you hear

Track
69

Tracks 60-69

Write the matching letter

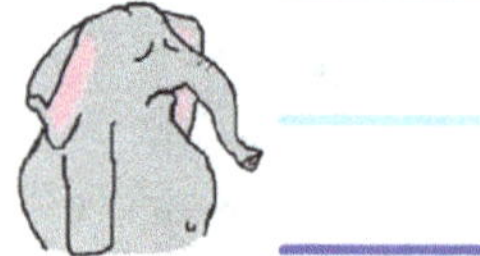 _______  _______  _______  _______

Chant

Track
70

New words: one   by   fella (fellow)

Sad tiger sits
Under the sun,
Tiger tears, tiger tears,
One by one.

Sad tiger sits
Under an umbrella,
Violins! Violins!
Sad, sad fella.

Story

Circle the sound you hear

Tracks 70-79

1. s t u v   2. s t u v

3. s t u v   4. s t u v

5. s t u v   6. s t u v

Listen and read along

New sight words: say go to win

Listen, point, and make the sound

Track 73

Tracks 70-79

W w   X x   Y y   Z z

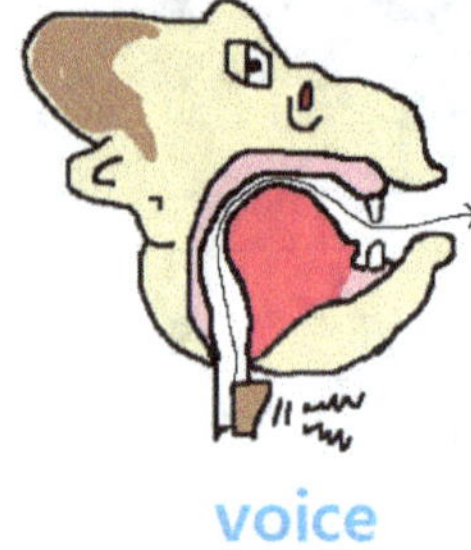
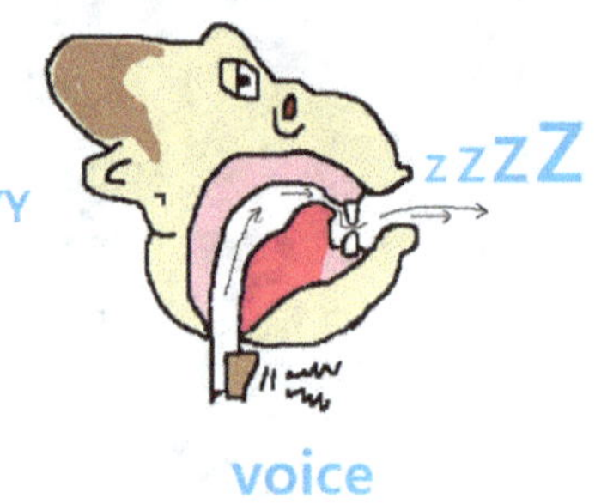

Listen and draw a line from the sound to the matching picture

w   x   y   z

Follow the rules

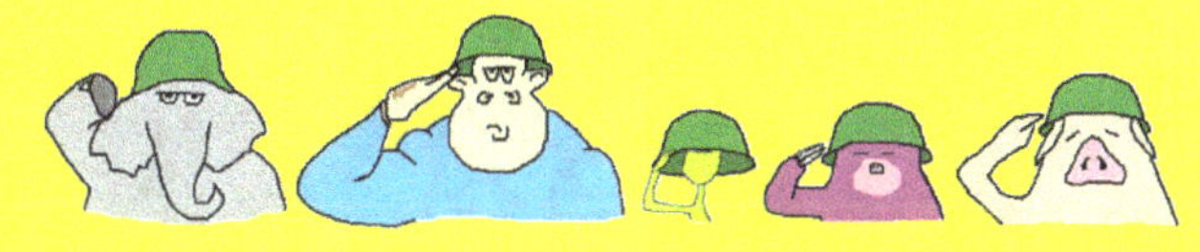

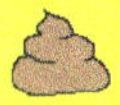

W W W W W

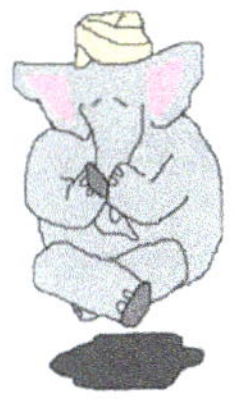

w w w w w w w

X X X X X

x x x x x x x

Y Y Y Y Y

y y y y y y y

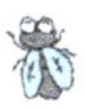

Z Z Z Z Z

z z z z z z z

New Words

Listen, point and repeat the new words 
Track 75

Ww

water   wave   window   wish

Xx

box   fix   fox   six

Yy

yawn   yellow   young   yo yo

Zz

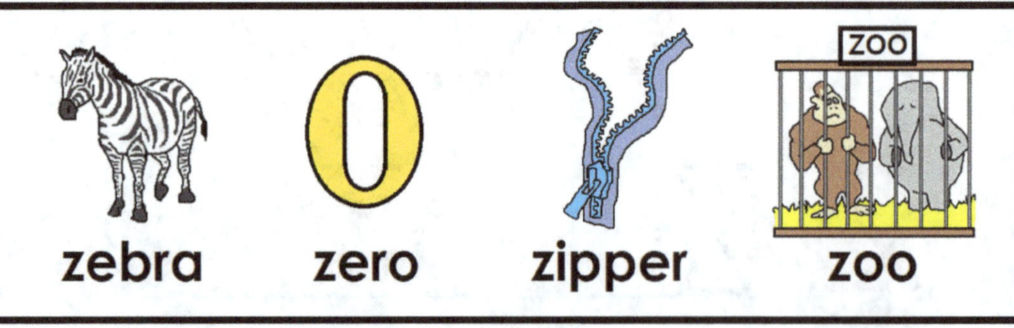

zebra   zero   zipper   zoo

Do it again..and again.. and again!

Exercises

Writing practice

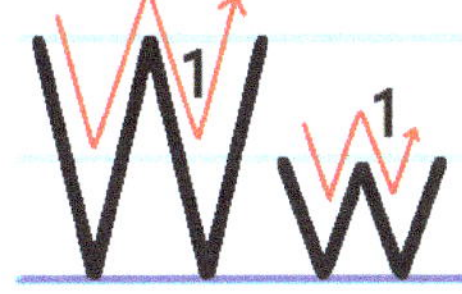

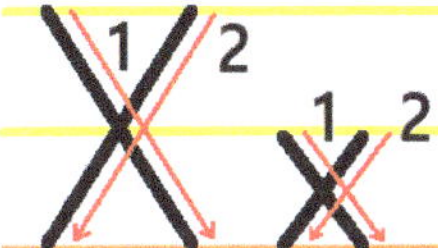

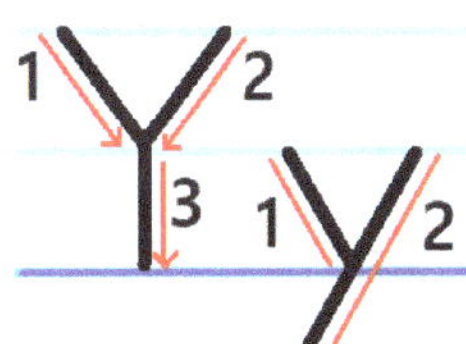

Word search *Listen and circle the word you hear*

Tracks 70-79

window   zero   young   wave   yellow   zipper   yo-yo   box

fix   zebra   zoo   water   fox   yawn   six   wish

Exercises

Circle the word you hear

Write the matching letter

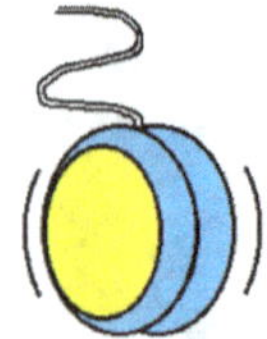 _____  6 _____  _____  _____

Chant

New sight words: I   had   it

I wish I had a zebra,
I wish I had a fox,
I wish I had a yo yo,
All in a yellow box,
I wish I did,
I wish I did,
I wish it had a yellow lid!

Story

Circle the sound you hear

1. w x y z
2. w x y z
3. w x y z
4. w x y z
5. w x y z
6. w x y z

Listen and read along

New sight words: wait

Review

Track 81

Tracks 80-89

Listen, point, and say

M m

N n

O o

P p

Q q

R r

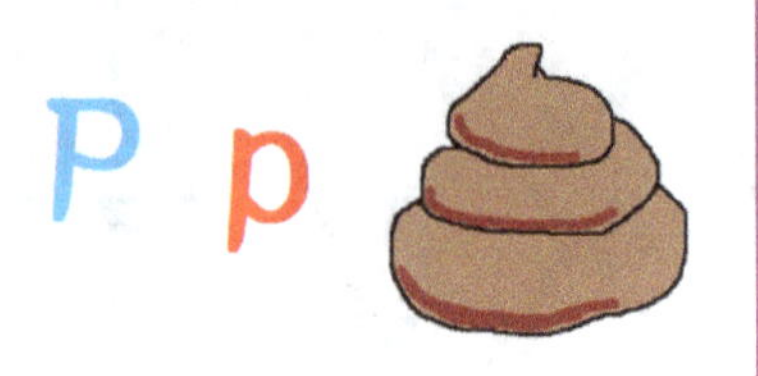

S s

T t

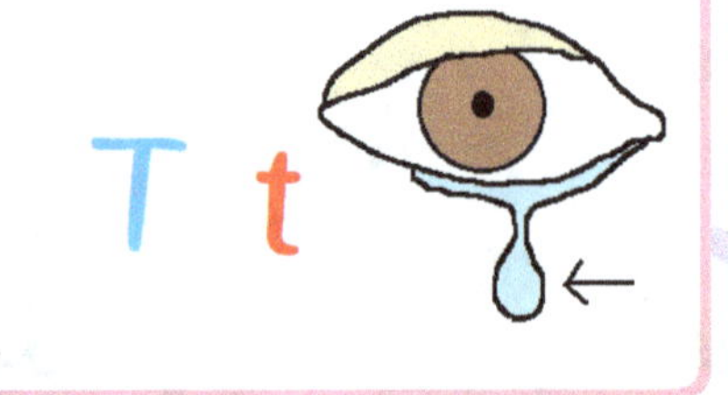

U u

V v

W w

X x

Y y

Z z

Review

Say all the words and write the letters

  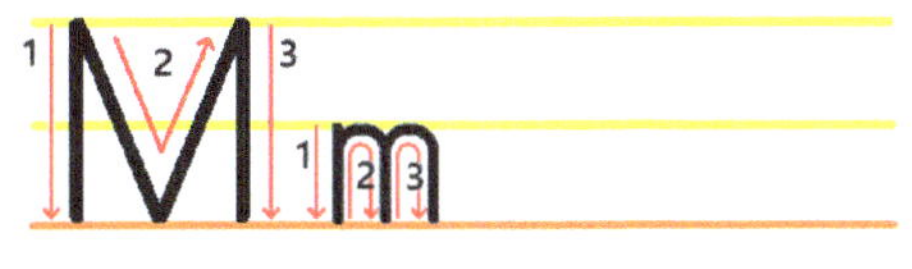
M m

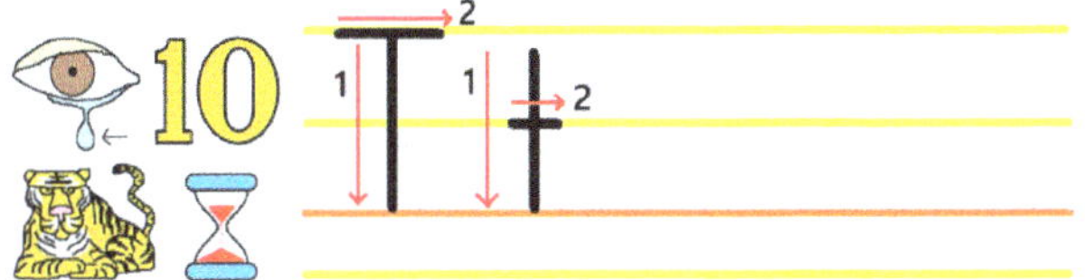
T t

N n

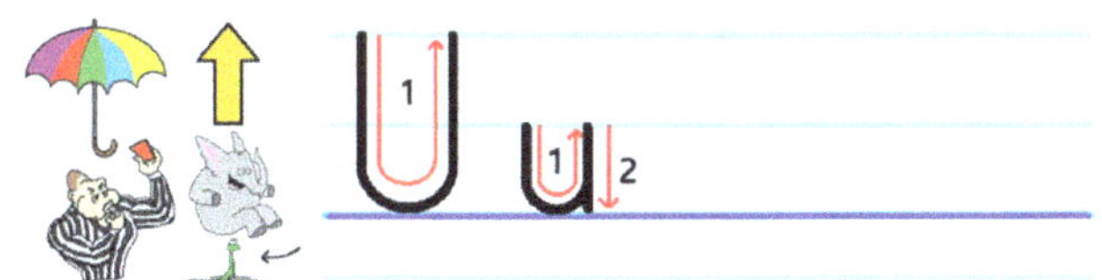
U u

O o

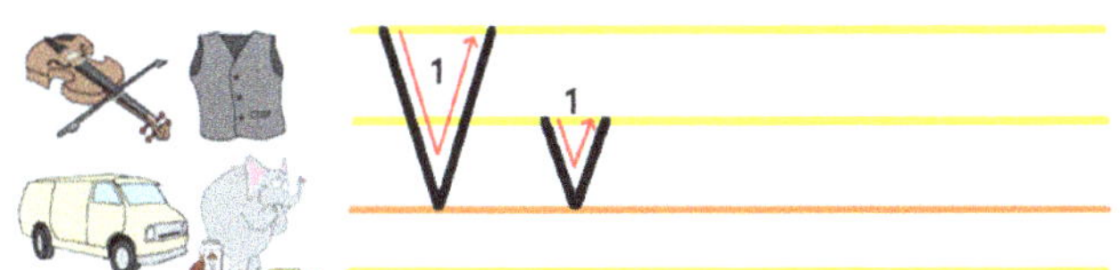
V v

 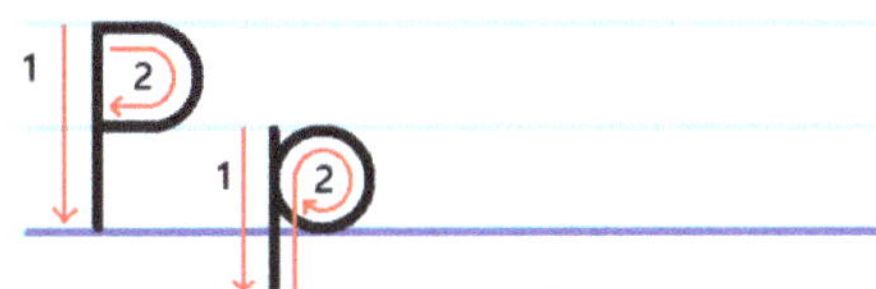
P p

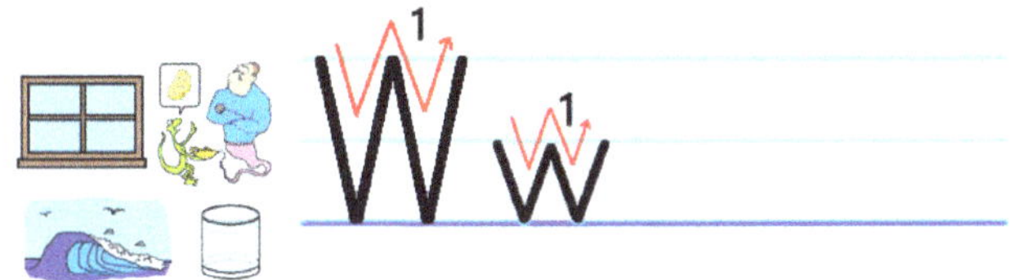
W w

 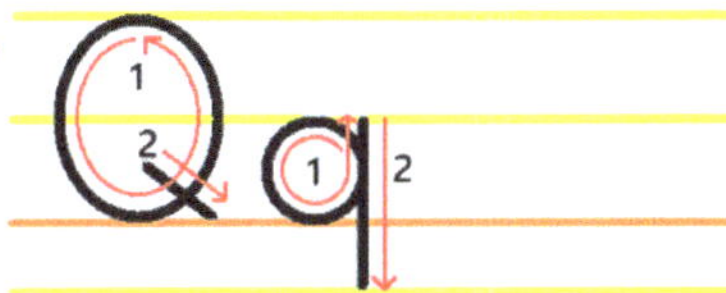
Q q

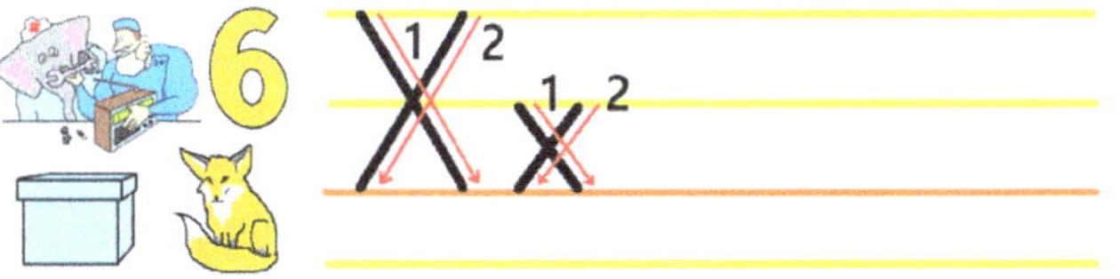
X x

 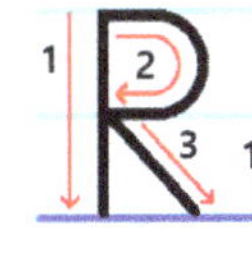
R r

Y y

 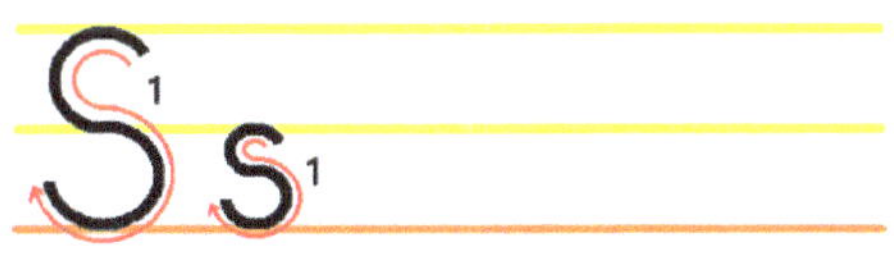
S s

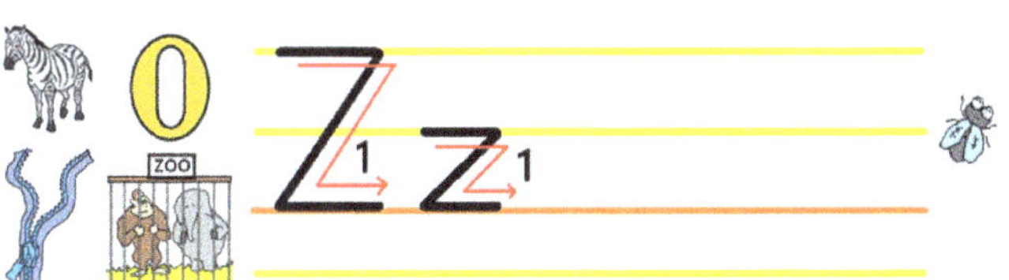
Z z

Review

Find the path

1 **M**     **r**

2 **R**    **t**

3 **T**    **m**

4 **U**     **y**

5 **Y** 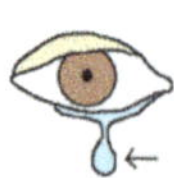    **u**

Listen and circle the matching letter

Track 82

Tracks 80-89

1		m s v	2		p s z
3		r n t	4		y u w
5	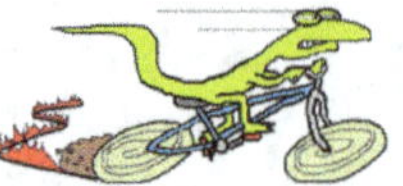	o q x	6		m t p
7		t r q	8		x z v

Review

Write the word twice

1 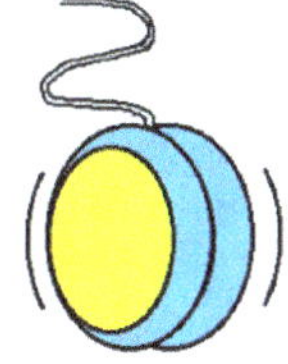

2 

3 

4 

5 

6 

Review

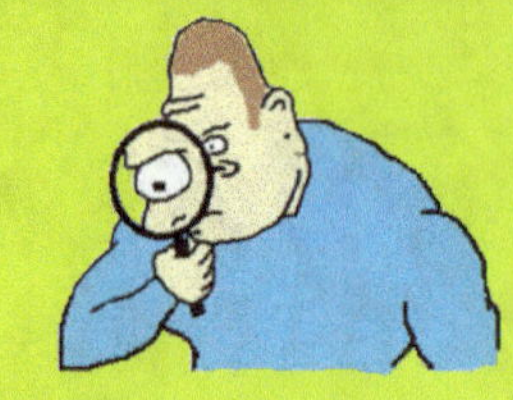

Listen, find, and circle

Track 83

Tracks 80-89

1 bird 2 egg 3 run 4 candy 5 milk 6 zebra 7 fish 8 vomit 9 door 10 hat
11 gold 12 jam 13 wave 14 nail 15 time 16 poop 17 ostrich 18 kangaroo
19 lemon 20 insect 21 monkey 22 angry 23 queen 24 smell 25 under 26 yellow

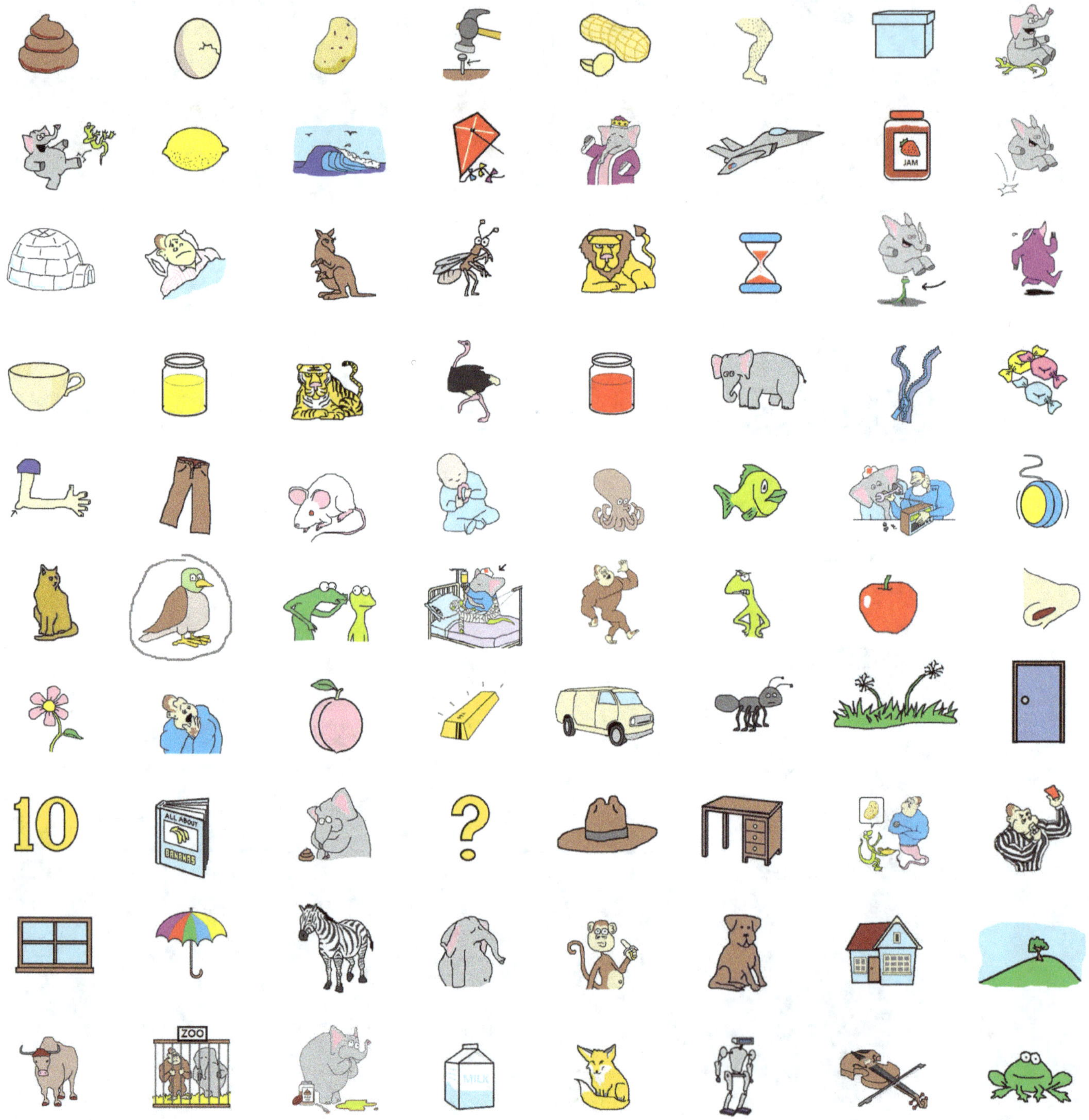

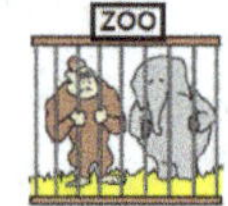

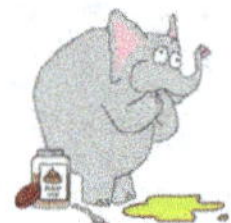

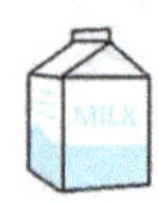

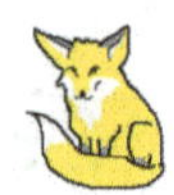

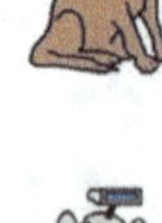

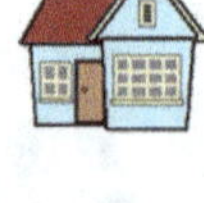

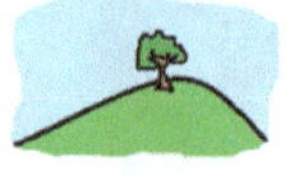

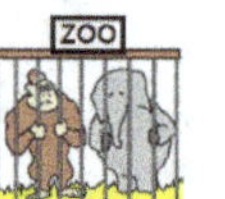

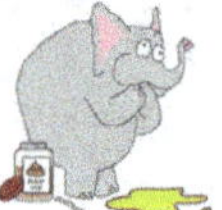

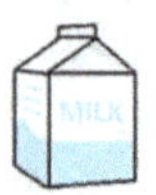

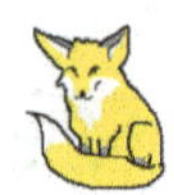

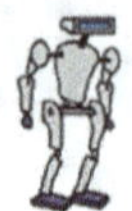

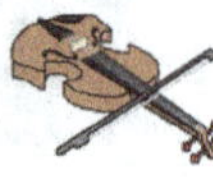

Review

Find the wrong ones and cross them out
(Say the first letter of each word... is it right?)

1

    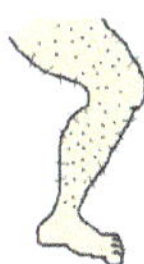

cup   six   potato   four   leg

2

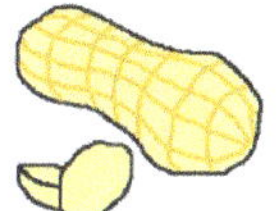    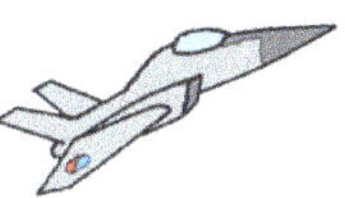

nut   flower   zebra   igloo   jet

3

wave   gorilla   kick   house   kite

4

 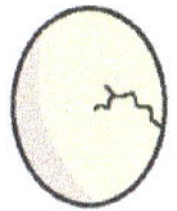   

jump   zoo   fox   kangaroo   lemon

5

mouse   queen   banana   lion   in

6

car   jam   moon   time   insect

Test

Listen and circle the word you hear a  b  c 

1       

2       

3       

4      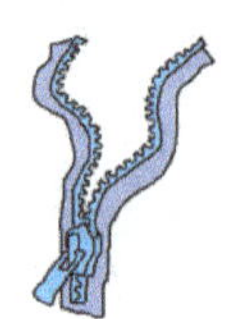 

5    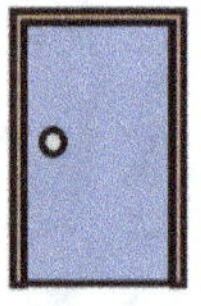  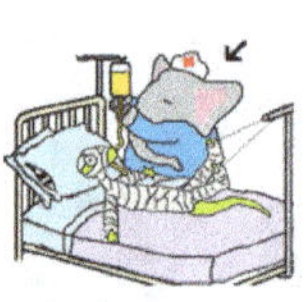 

6 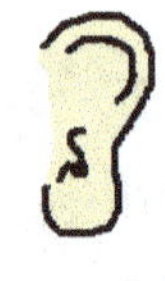      

7   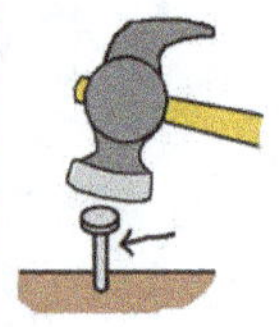 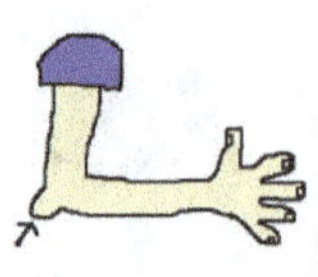   

Test

Listen and write the sound you hear a  b  c 

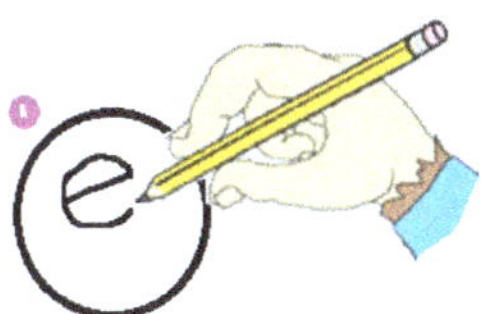

Tracks 80-89

1	2	3	4
5	6	7	8
9	10	11	12
13	14	15	16

Test

Write the letter to match the picture

 1
 2
 3

 4
 5
 6

 7
 8
 9

 10
 11
 12

 13
 14
 15

Test

Listen and circle the sound you hear   a [Track 90] b [Track 91] c [Track 92]

Tracks 90-93

1  j c f w o

2  a g n d i

3  o h x s l

4  u b e z q

5  p k m r a

6  h y v t g

CONGRATULATIONS!!

Now you know your alphabet sounds..

You can sing the

Alphabet Sound Song!!

Listen and sing along..if you can!   Track 93   Tracks 90-93

a b c d e f g

h i j k 

l m n o p 

q r s t u v

w x y and z

How did you do?

This is the end
of the book!

Word List

Unit 1

alligator

angry

ant

apple

baby

banana

bird

book

candy

car

cat

cup

Unit 2

desk

diamond

dog

door

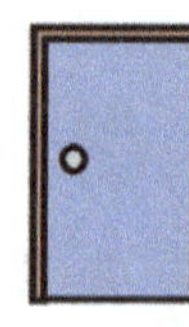

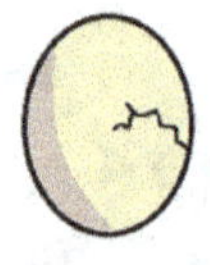
egg

elbow

elephant

elf

fish

flower

four

frog

Word List

Unit 3

gold

good

gorilla

grass

happy

hat

hill

house

igloo

ill

in

insect

Unit 4

jail

jam

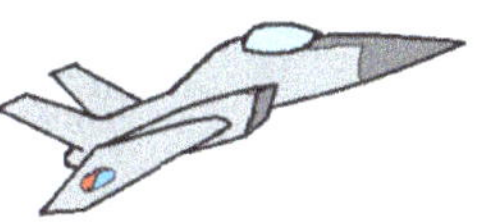
jam

jump

kangaroo

key

kick

kite

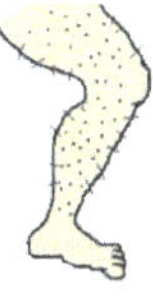
leg

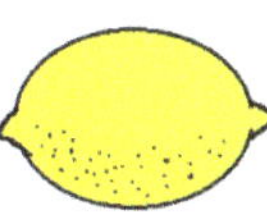
lemon

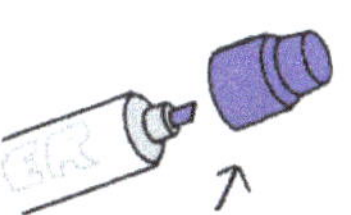
lid

lion

Word List

Unit 5

milk

monkey

moon

mouse

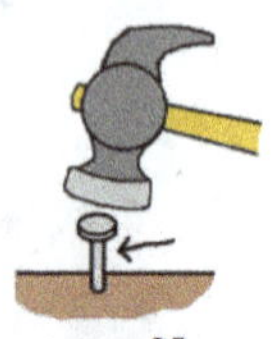

nail

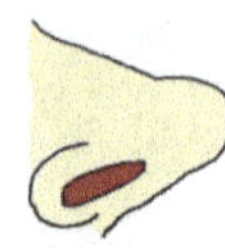

nose

nurse

nut

octopus

old

ostrich

ox

Unit 6

pants

peach

poop

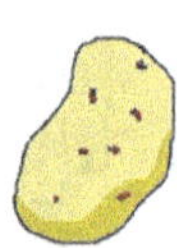

potato

queen

question

quick

quiet

radio

red

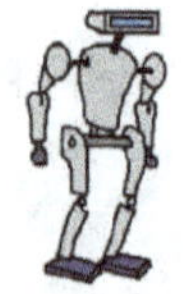

robot

run

Word List

Unit 7

sad

sit

smell

sun

tear

ten

tiger

time

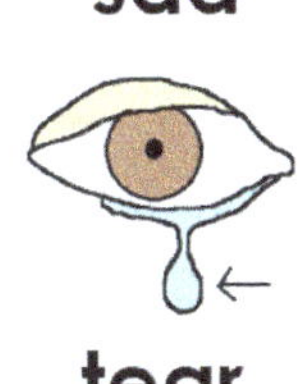
umbrella

umpire

under

up

van

vest

violin

vomit

Unit 8

water

wave

window

wish

box

fix

fox

six

yawn

yellow

young

yo yo

zebra

zero

zipper

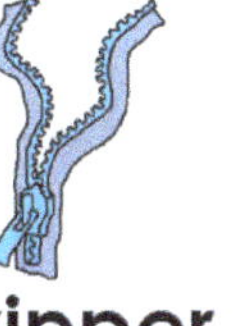
zoo

Our Sight Words

	Word	Note (ESL)		Word	Note (ESL)
P16	a/an			by	
	and			fellow	
P22	all			say	
	on			go	
	in			to	
	the			win	
P29	no		P64	I	
P34	lift			had	
	like			it	
	get			wait	
P46	oh				
	not				
P52	did				
	you				
	your				
	yes				
	my				
	has				
	put				
P58	one				

OUR SIGHT WORD FLASH CARDS!

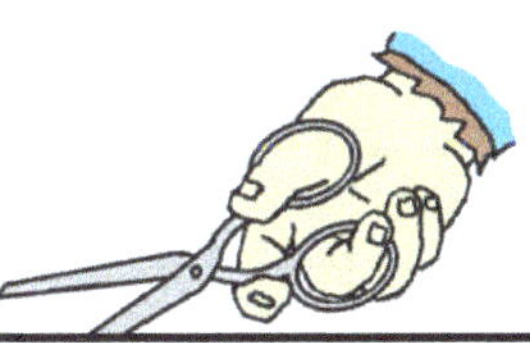

a/an	and
all	on
in	the
no	lift

OUR SIGHT WORD FLASH CARDS!

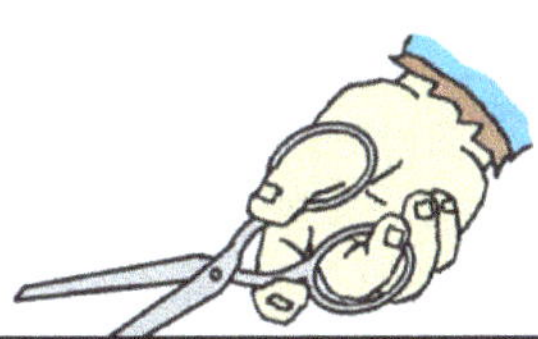

like	get
oh	not
did	you
your	yes

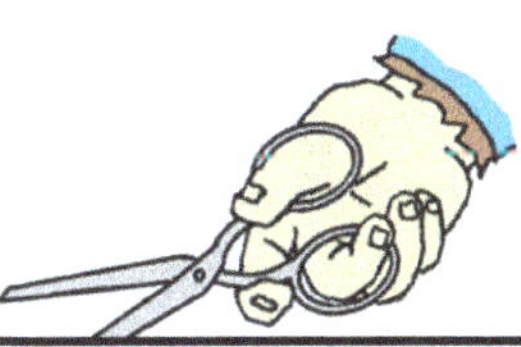

my	has
put	one
by	fellow
say	go

OUR SIGHT WORD FLASH CARDS!

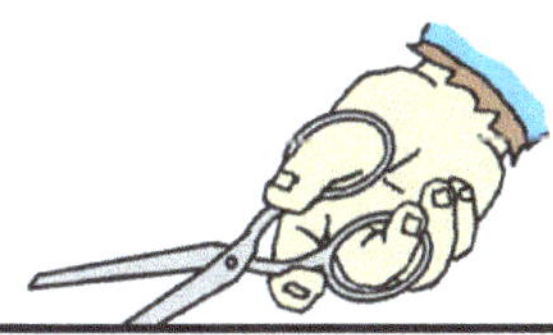

to	win
I	had
it	wait

Phonics Series

Preschool:

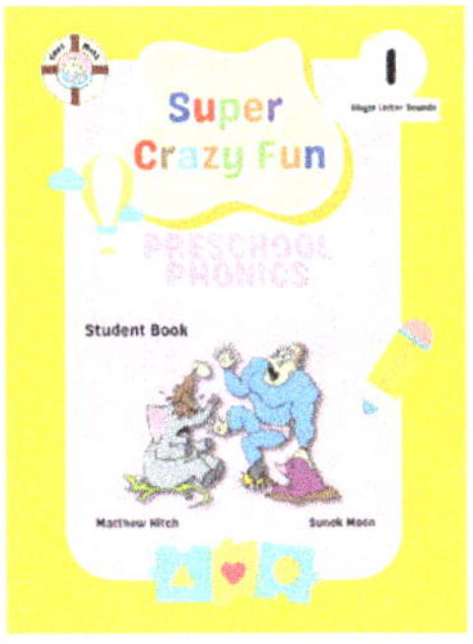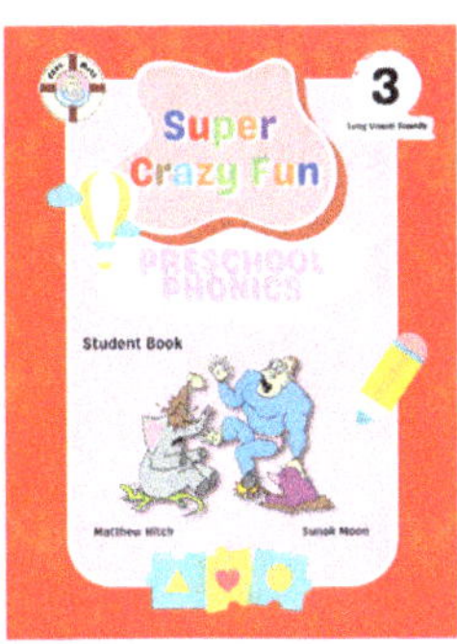

Kindergarten:

Elementary School Junior:

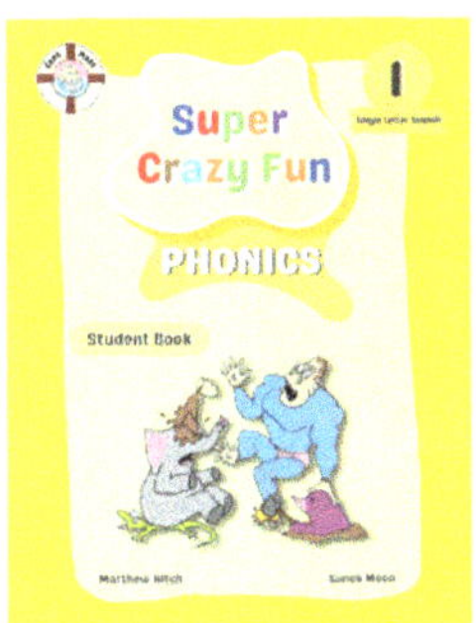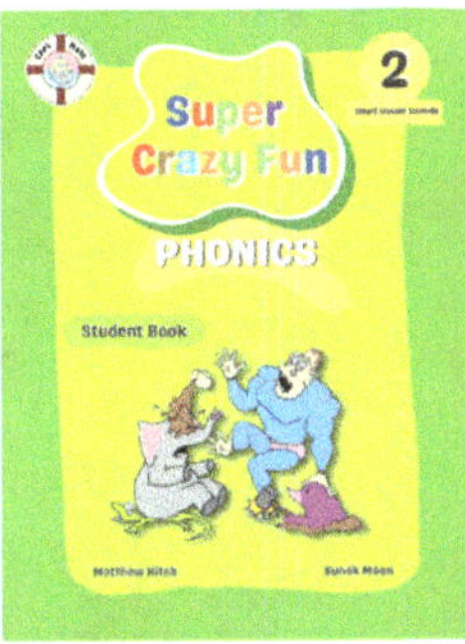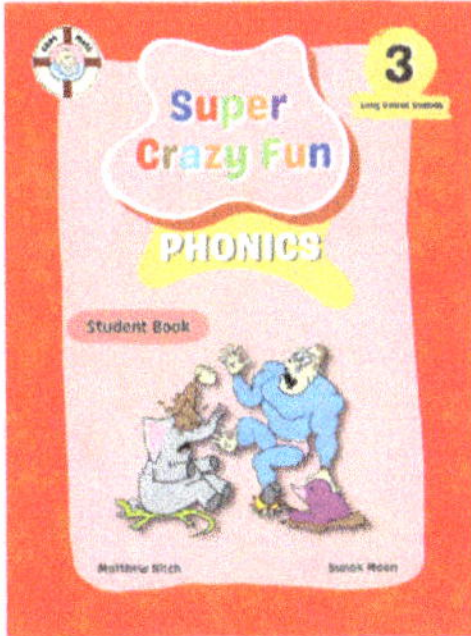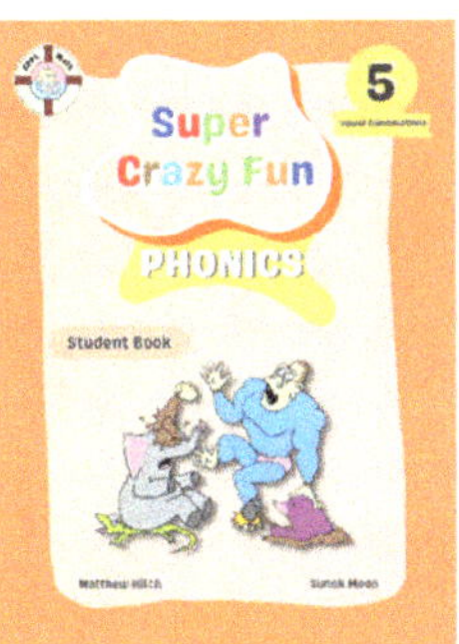

Elementary School Senior/Remedial:

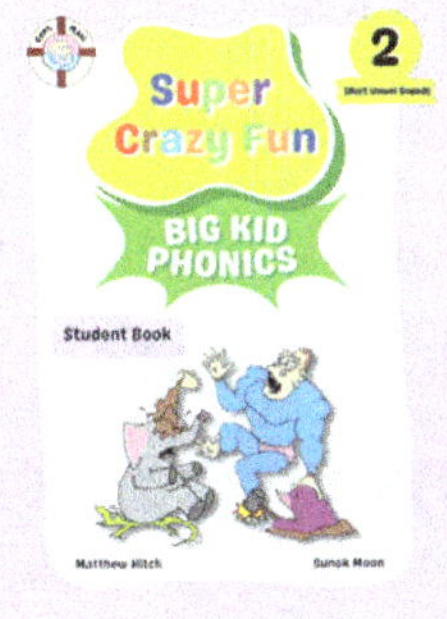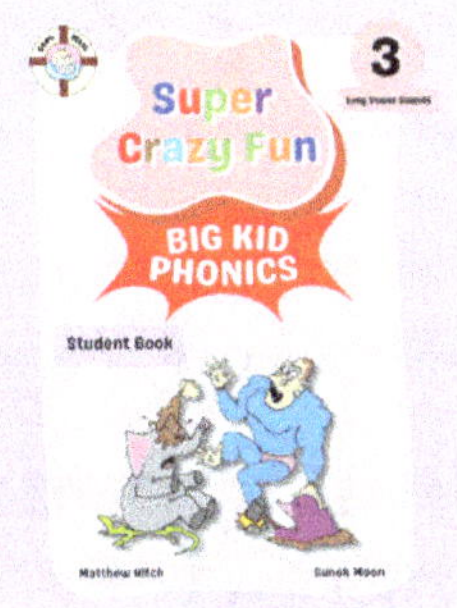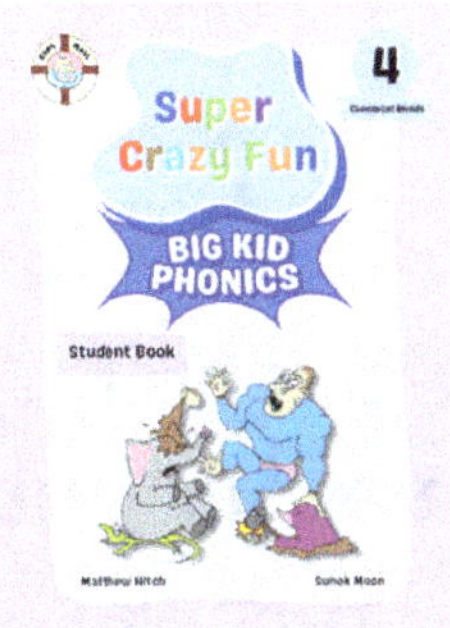

Incidentally, the contents of all these phonics books are available in one big silly book, too:

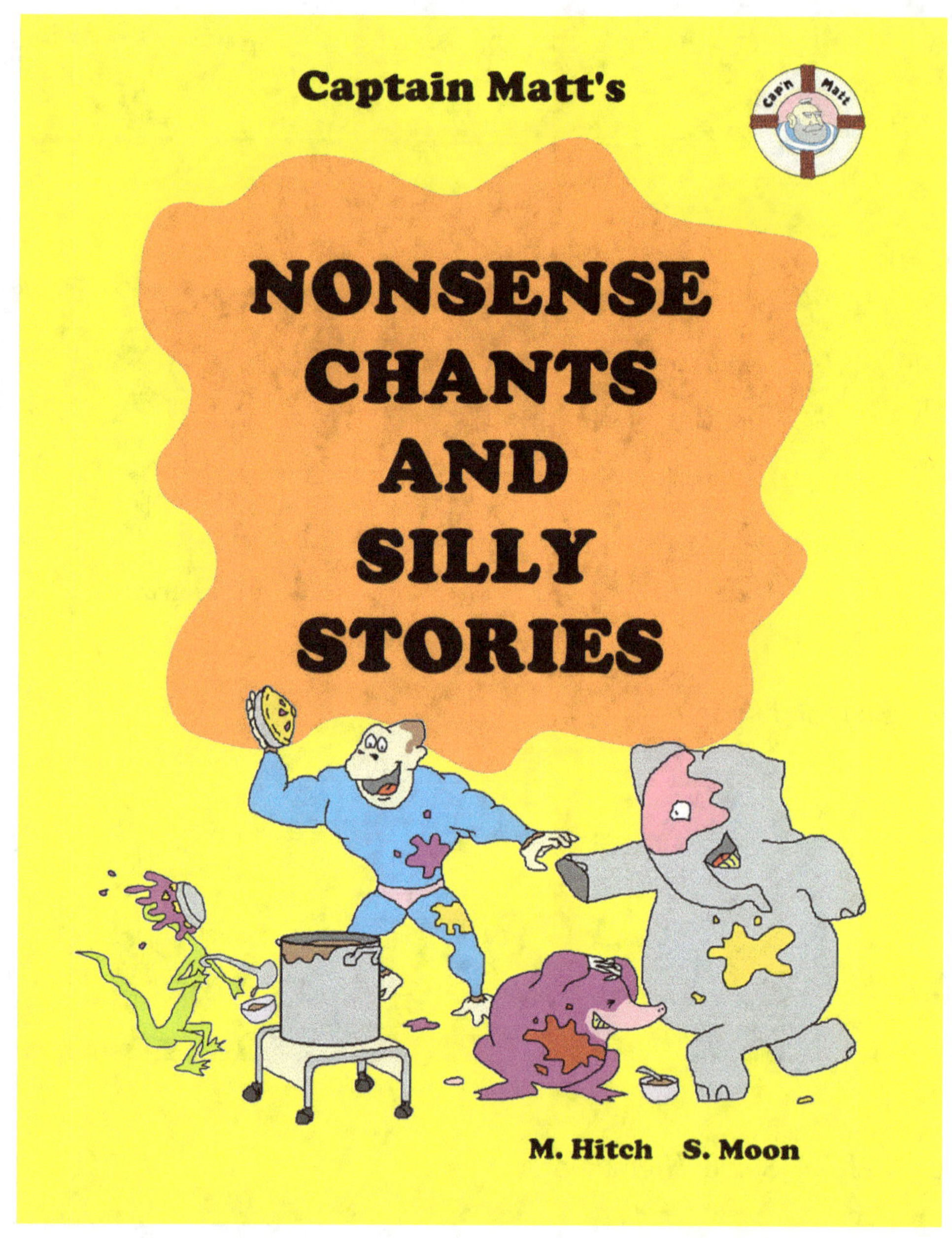

Have a look in Amazon or check our website: www.supercrazyfun.net (or just search online in case our publishing options have increased since this was printed.)

25 103 210	0 102 255	0 91 158	63 72 204	0 0 204	0 0 255	68 134 255	0 72 204		14 49 190	0 72 204	14 49 190	57 53 238	20 16 188	0 0 222	22 92 188	219 36 60

62 2 202	104 40 253	99 31 226	91 6 176	131 68 176	255 0 255	173 68 200	199 69 196		255 128 255	255 0 255	255 128 192	255 108 156	255 83 169	245 114 153	235 95 175	240 117 197

255 0 0	255 0 19	222 33 52	237 18 95	219 36 60	238 32 94	242 60 6	237 81 35		254 96 1	255 115 0	243 125 29	252 149 46	255 145 77	253 181 83	255 255 123	244 225 89

251 238 0 *	240 228 11	255 255 0	255 247 91	239 250 44	228 241 65	194 235 71	151 228 35		53 217 102	90 186 74	20 224 158	3 241 211	3 134 190	66 99 191	12 81 243	27 82 226